# HOSEA HOUSE

## AN OVERCOMER'S GUIDE WHEN SOMEONE
## YOU LOVE IS AN ADDICT

PEGGY L. WATSON

CROSSBOOKS®
PUBLISHING

CrossBooks™
A Division of LifeWay
One LifeWay Plaza
Nashville, TN 37234
www.crossbooks.com
Phone: 1-866-768-9010

First published by CrossBooks  09/09/2014

ISBN: 978-1-4627-5230-0 (sc)
ISBN: 978-1-4627-5231-7 (hc)
ISBN: 978-1-4627-5229-4 (e)

Library of Congress Control Number: 2014914176

Printed in the United States of America.

This book is printed on acid-free paper.

# CONTENTS

For my husband, Lonnie—a conqueror through Christ!

# FOREWORD

I have friends, or had friends, who lost everything. Some even lost their lives. I have one wonderful friend who lost everything to his gambling addiction. It started with a seemingly innocent two-dollar lottery ticket. He would purchase one or two tickets a day at first, but before long he was spending fifty dollars or more a day. When that didn't feel exciting enough, the horse or dog tracks were the natural place to land, trying to win big, to make up for all the money lost to the lottery. It was more exciting, and lots of people liked it, too. Exciting that is, until his two homes, his business, and his cars all became the property of someone else.

Most people, even churchgoing folks, will tell you, "No, I don't have any addictions. I have never been addicted to anything." But talk to them long enough, and they might tell you about the pain pills the doctor first prescribed two years ago, saying, "Well, they make me feel good and help with other pains I have, too." They may be unwilling or unable to recognize their own issues, yet all the while think how their child, their brother, or their sister's kid sure has a problem.

Addiction is a strange bedfellow. It's the thing that keeps guys going to their fishing hole, golfers going to the course. It's the one that got away. It's the one shot made on the fourteenth hole just like Phil Mickelson or Tiger Woods. It's the rush or feeling that takes us away from who and where we are, if only for a brief time. One person's addiction to drugs, alcohol, or gambling has the ability to destroy not only the user, but also the user's family, as well as anyone who loves or is particularly close to that user. No one—not a husband, wife, mother, father, son, daughter, grandchild, friend, or even business partner—is immune to the effects of their sickness. And it is a sickness, just as anything that is not in the will of our Lord and Savior Jesus Christ can be called a sickness. Jesus, the

Great Physician, said it best when he said those who are sick have need of a physician (Matthew 9:12).

My sickness wasn't prescription pain pills or lotto tickets. Years ago, from time to time I would buy a few lottery tickets when traveling about the country, especially when the jackpot was huge and others were in on it, too, but it just seemed crazy to me to spend ten or twenty dollars on a ticket that I was going to keep for a day or so and then throw in the trash. Besides, that was money I could use on my drug of choice—crack cocaine.

I never knew what a drug was or even tasted beer until age eighteen. I didn't like the thought of cocaine. I was an athlete, college-ready, with over a hundred college offers on the table. It happened at a big private party, at a big house in an exclusive subdivision. *I'll do it once, and if I don't like it I'll quit*, I thought. I made the choice to use freebase crack cocaine to go along with most everyone else there. I later tried to explain to someone who had never used it, "It's like taking the devil by the tail just for fun, only now he isn't letting go, and it's not fun anymore." Not all those who get caught up in drugs or alcohol like it. You see, I was raised in church, and it had taught me, "We don't talk about things like drug addiction." In my first seventeen years, I never missed a service. So when I was in my forties and I started going to a group meeting, I didn't see how their solution in a church classroom would work for me. But the group leader and those attending the meeting were so open and honest and they said the things I wanted to say but didn't dare.

I had enough self-awareness most days to see what I was doing on my own wasn't working. I wanted to be cured of the trouble that came with the addiction, but to be honest, I didn't really want to give up the part my brain liked (because of the things the drug was doing in my brain—I know that now). The very thing my brain was telling me it needed and wanted was the very thing that was killing me and making my life a miserable wreck. My brain would say to me, "It's good, I like it." But it was only getting worse, to the point that my brain had decided the solution was to check out of everything, end this life as I knew it, be done with it all. Trying to kill myself didn't work, and now I'm glad it didn't. My eyes have been opened to a whole new way to live, which I could never get a handle on before. The God that was always so talked about in church, but rarely seen, loved me and would come to me just as I am. And, to all those who are willing, he will come into those lives and make the changes that need to be made, but only under his conditions. A new way of living in Christ was made available to me, and I have a reason for being here.

I haven't used cocaine of any type now for fourteen years, and I don't have any desire to. I'm not foolish enough to think I quit it on my own. All glory to God our Father, and I praise him for a wife who loved me so much she would not give me up. She got me to a place where there were people who were so openly honest about their issues and just as honest about the cure—Jesus Christ. By the way, my friend who lost everything to gambling now has his life back, his family, a good job, and a new home. He would tell you the same thing: "You've got to deal in truth, and the only truth is God's Word." It's not open for debate. Humanity's opinions are just that—three steps to this, five steps to that. I say one step. Meet your creator to ask that his plan be brought forth in you: "'For I know the plans I have for you,' says the Lord. 'They are plans for good and not for disaster, to give you a future and a hope'" (Jeremiah 29:11 NLT).

Over the past decade, I have been asked to talk with many different individuals struggling with addiction. One common thread is this: the addict is not the only mess. The whole family is largely a mess too. I have found a big part of the family's time is consumed with talking about and wondering what they're going to do with their addict. By the time these addictions start to show their ugly heads, it's usually deeper than first confession. We learn that the "little problem" is anything but little. A person really lost his or her job because of going in late or not at all, or due to a failed drug test. The car we were first told doesn't run may now be in hock at the local title place or local drug dealer for the bargain price of three hundred dollars, never mind you paid three thousand for it. The addict said he or she would make the payments if you would sign for it, because something happened, out of his or her control that hurt his or her credit, but he or she was good for it. *Yeah! Right!*

Just don't be surprised when the facts of their stories change or get fuzzy each time the stories are told. At the point when the truth finally surfaces, anger is usually unleashed by the addict, who is trying to protect his or her way of life. After all, few people would hand over two or three hundred or a thousand dollars to a person if they were openly honest and said, "Hey, I've been on a bad losing streak at the track. Would you let me have a few hundred, and when I get a lucky streak going, I'll pay you back." Or, "I don't have any cash, and I was hoping to catch a buzz. I only need a few hundred dollars and a place to crash for a while."

Addicts will use every emotion possible—from tears to tantrums—to get the outcome they want, to keep their addiction alive. Sadly, too many loved ones give in to the addict's hustle just to have some peace for a time, just so they will go away. But guess what? They come back! And now they have no home, no job, no money, no car, and usually lots of needs, like doctor appointments, court dates, outstanding tickets, arrest warrants, etc. Why on earth do we allow people who manage their own affairs so badly make decisions that affect our finances, our lives, and, in the end, turn everything upside down? Addiction will die only when you kill it! If you're feeding it at all, at any level, it won't die. If it's alive, it is being fed. We wouldn't dream of telling a loved one who has cancer, "Well, here; let's do something that will keep the cancer living and growing."

For purposes of time and paper, let me just say that if your way of *fixing* your addict isn't working, then stop it! Just stop! Not one more, "Well, maybe if I just …" If you truly want help for your addict, you must get help yourself.

This book guides you using God's words and plans for you, so you can be victorious in daily living. When life's battles are raging and we don't know what to do anymore, God will raise a standard up that relieves us of any fear or worry in all situations. It ministers to the person dealing with the aftermath of the addict's storm. Almost every person in church is or has been dealing with this very issue. Sadly, too many Christians do not read their Bible during the week, nor do they know how to apply God's word to their new lives in Christ. This book will help loved ones and pastors to rightly apply God's word to the specific situation of addiction. With so many families dealing with addiction, it can save untold hours in trying to meet the individual needs of almost every member of the body of Christ who is searching for answers. I hope all pastors in all churches will have multiple copies of this book in his or their offices.

Let me say thank you, thank you, thank you so much to Jesus my Savior, who loved me so much he chose to die in my place and give me the life he planned for me all along. It's only by his grace, nothing I did to earn it, nothing I can do to keep it. It's all because of him, and his mercy, and his love for me. And thank you, Peggy, for allowing God to use you to bring his sweet Spirit and comfort to whosoever will.

Lonnie Watson

# ACKNOWLEDGMENTS

This book would never have been written without my husband's struggle with addiction. Through those hard years, I have my God and my Savior, Jesus Christ, the champion of my soul to thank. Truly, without his hand guiding me to the sure place I now rest, I would still be lost, adrift, and helpless. Thank you, God, for rescuing me! In hindsight, I realize God wishes to use those years to bring the light of hope to those who are currently living in the grip of addiction. So I thank my husband for that particular ride over the cliff that I might experience and know the saving hand of Christ is real. I'm eternally grateful for my husband's loving and supportive enthusiasm for this project! I love you, Lonnie!

I wish to thank faithful friends, Al and Rita Gambil, and David Lamb, for walking beside us on our broken road. Thank you for never judging, always loving, and talking straight with us. Tough love is the best love; Rita and David taught me this. Fearless love is necessary when dealing with addiction; Al taught me this. I'll never forget how you changed your plans and drove me two hours to get my car back after Lonnie had taken off in it. Oh, the stories we could tell about those years! Thank you for your encouragement, prayers, music, and time. You were selfless, Rita. I needed you more than you knew, and you never disappointed me. You were the one who suggested what I was writing down should become a book. I imagine you are rejoicing with us from heaven seeing this book in print. One day, we will meet again!

I wish to also thank Julie Hearne, who spent time helping to edit this book. Thank you for challenging me to make it better, for having the nerve to offer critiques knowing this project was near and dear to my heart. You are brave, dear friend!

To all those who encouraged me over the years with teaching and writing; my heart is full. You know who you are. I love you all!

> All praise to God, the Father of our Lord Jesus Christ. God is our merciful Father and the source of all comfort. He comforts us in all our troubles so that we can comfort others. When they are troubled, we will be able to give them the same comfort God has given us. (2 Corinthians 1:3–4 NLT)

# WHO IS THE MODERN-DAY HOSEA?

Are you the loved one of an addict?
You are labeled as *Hosea* throughout this book.

Are you an addict?
This book refers to you as *Gomer*.

Who is your Gomer? Perhaps your spouse is your Gomer. Your Gomer could be your teenager or your adult child. Your Gomer could even be your best friend. To me, when you have an addict in your life whose destructive habits are corrosive to your own life, health, emotional well-being, finances, etc., then that person is your Gomer. Often we Hoseas are willing to go down the destructive path along with our Gomers, because we love them. That is why this book appeals to you, right? That is what is making you want to read this book. And you pray this book has answers.

These terms are meant to be gender and age neutral, so they include men, women, boys, and girls. And although I have also chosen to use male pronouns throughout the book (he, his, etc.), I did so for ease of writing and reading purposes. These references are not meant in any way to exclude females or diminish the female gender. Please view these pronouns as gender neutral.

I didn't start out writing a book. When I discovered my husband was an addict, I looked for books to help me, but I didn't find any. I was left only frustrated. Everything I found was based on helping the addict. Nothing out there was just for me. I was drowning. Lonnie may never clean up! Where was my help? Who had advice for me?

You can tell people to walk away and don't look back, but that's not really a solution for the loved one of an addict. The problem is that we do love them. Walking away is not a realistic solution. Even if we do physically separate, the heart is still troubled and tangled up with them. So I began to write down thoughts, tips to help me, Scriptures that encouraged me, etc. One day a friend asked was I was doing, and I let her read what I had written so far. She began to cry. Her husband was already recovered, but she said she wished she'd had this information during the hardest times. She is the one who suggested it become a book. Thank you, Rita!

Here is a bit of our story:

Beginning in 1994, I started dealing with addiction—not my own but rather my husband's addiction to crack cocaine. He used other drugs, too, including alcohol and marijuana, but his real love was crack. In 1999, while driving down the road to find my husband, who had been gone a couple of days on a drug binge, I heard a gospel bluegrass song by the Isaacs entitled, "I've Come to Take You Home." Through the lyrics of this song, I found a personal connection with the story of Hosea, a minor prophet in the Old Testament. For the first time, my emotional roller coaster was summed up in a matter of three verses and a chorus. I pulled to the side of the road and sobbed uncontrollably. I encourage you to listen to the Isaacs sing this song on YouTube or iTunes. The lyrics can easily be found on the Internet.

The Lord gave us a special blessing eleven years later, when in the summer of 2010 The Isaacs played a concert at the church we were attending. It was very emotional for me to meet this group and to share my story with them in person. They had no idea the song they sang described the life of an addict so perfectly or had played such a huge part in my personal healing. I will always be grateful to them for taking the time to listen to my story and share in my life that way.

Now here's the condensed Bible story of Hosea:

The story opens with Hosea being told to marry a prostitute named Gomer. After the wedding, she gives birth to three children. Hosea discovers in chapter 2 that Gomer has been unfaithful during their marriage, sleeping with many other lovers. Hosea never stopped loving

Gomer, but he couldn't tolerate what she was doing. Eventually Gomer leaves Hosea and returns to prostitution, which leads her into slavery and bondage. By chapter 3 we find that some time has passed when one day Hosea hears about a group of slaves being sold. He goes to the slave market in the hopes of redeeming Gomer (buying her back), as the Lord told him to do. There she was! By law, in Hosea's time, he could have ordered her death, which she expected, and many in Hosea's time would have said she deserved it. But Hosea purchased her in love in order to give her a good life and take her back home.

While this story is very much the story of God's love toward humankind in that he sent his only Son, Jesus, to die on the cross in order to redeem us, it also demonstrates the agony that one goes through when a loved one is an addict. While my husband didn't sleep around like Gomer did, he did slip around to use crack. Crack was his lover, his mistress. It was how he spent his time and money. He became so engulfed in it, that he might as well have been considered its slave. He all but forsook our marriage for the substance as he slowly turned into someone I barely knew and truthfully didn't like.

If you are like me, the news of your Gomer's addiction came as a real shock. I wasn't completely naïve; after all, a husband doesn't stay gone for days on end nearly every week unless there is a problem. Our finances had taken a severe plunge, too, in recent months, but since my husband and his brother owned their own business (there were no paychecks), he explained it away, saying the business wasn't doing well anymore. I didn't have a clue how much money was missing until much later.

"There's no easy way to tell you, so I'll just say it," was my husband's reply when I demanded to know what was going on. "I'm addicted to crack cocaine." He didn't look at me. He said it flat and dry.

My reaction was equally emotionless. The weeks leading up to this revelation had already taken all our emotions away. There were none left to erupt. We talked intermittently for the next couple of hours. My first question was whether or not he wanted to quit or continue. He cried, saying that he wanted off of it. "Do you still love me?" he asked with pain in his eyes. Of course I did. I was hurting deeply, but my love for him hadn't gone away completely. It had merely crawled into a ball in the corner to protect itself from any more blows. It crept out slowly and then embraced him like a mother would embrace her terminally ill child.

So there it was. He was addicted. He wanted to stop.

We still loved each other. It was just a matter of his quitting.

I would help him.

There.

With that settled, I took a deep breath of relief. Needless to say, I knew nothing about drug addiction. I had personally never used a single illegal drug in my life! I knew when we married that he had used drugs in his past, but I didn't realize their long tentacles could reach forward into a user's future and poison it, too. I wasn't prepared for the future of ups and downs, broken promises, and endless nights of tears. I didn't know how often I would scream in the solitude of my own disastrous life.

When you too are tired of living in the ruins of your shattered life, put to use the principles you will find in this book. I can't take away the rubble, but I can help you figure out how to clean it up for yourself using God's principles. I can't make your loved one stop using any more than I could make my husband stop using, but I can help you reclaim your life, your peace of mind, and your own stability. After all, that's what's missing.

Lonnie didn't change overnight, and although he has learned how to defeat crack through God's strength, he must fight against it on a regular basis. Our story is not over, nor will it be so long as we live, but the years have given me wisdom I want to share to perhaps help others deal with the insanity of a loved one's addiction.

I know there are many other Hoseas out there suffering as they watch their Gomers—husbands, wives, sons, daughters, siblings, or even close friends—addicted to a substance. It's pure agony when you try to help, giving all that you have attempting to somehow reach them, and all your efforts seem futile. This book is about hope, peace, and sanity—the three things we Hoseas long for yet struggle to maintain. I pray what I have gone through offers you help.

Part One of this book is to help you understand addiction in general and to give you tips on how to deal with your addict. Part Two, the majority of this book, is all about *you*. I remember all too well falling apart. I remember feeling all alone, destitute, and embarrassed. I remember crying more tears and screaming more screams than I even knew were possible. I remember what it was like to finally have the courage to tell someone the truth about what was happening in my life and have that person look at me like I was a leper. I remember struggling to find the help I needed. Even now, as I edit and reread this book in preparation for publication, these memories stir up deep emotions, and I sob from my belly remembering my life then. I consider your life now, and I pray for you.

For the time being, stop worrying quite so much about your Gomer. It's time you start working on healing *you*. There is no instant cure for you or your Gomer. There are no certain steps to follow. It's important that you read every chapter. If you choose to read around in this book, please be sure to read all the chapters. Read them more than once. Read them as often as you feel weak and miserable. They all go hand in hand, helping you learn to overcome and find that joyous, victorious life in Christ you are longing for.

You will find this book is full of scriptural references. Please, I beg of you, take the time to read the Scriptures for yourself. Don't rush through it. Take the time to really soak it up and learn from it. Use whichever Bible translation you prefer and understand. Pray as you read, and study the Scriptures. God will enlighten you with what you need.

May God richly bless you!
Peggy

# PART ONE
# UNDERSTANDING AND DEALING WITH THE ADDICT

# CHAPTER 1

# WHY IS IT SO HARD TO QUIT?

"He said he'd get help. I found several telephone numbers of places that can help him, but he hasn't made any calls. He said he'd call tomorrow."

Addiction involves four distinct aspects that are intricately woven together: chemical, psychological, cultural, and spiritual. The chemical aspect is what most of us think about when we think of addiction—the withdrawals, the cravings, and the mood swings. For instance, when we send an addict to "dry out," we are simply removing the addict from drug use, usually just long enough for the addict's physical body to be purged from the direct chemical effects of the drug.

Indeed, drying out is necessary, but it is *not* recovery. For recovery to last, the addict must also deal with the psychological aspect of his addiction—the underlying reasons or need for going through life in an emotional fog. In my experience, the addict's emotional well-being is extremely fragile, if not a total farce. This is where the last two aspects of addiction intertwine. Our culture, through movies and music, often promotes a moderate amount of drug use, proclaiming it to be chic, hip, cool, and fun. It's even expected. Everyone goes through a wild, rebellious time in their life, right? The warped feelings and thoughts of the addict are fueled by this cultural disposition, while a spiritual battle for the very soul of the addict (and every other human) is waging in heavenly places (Ephesians 6:12).

In order to better understand these four aspects of addiction and therefore be better equipped to grapple with your Gomer's problems, let's look deeper into each aspect one at a time. First, attempt to learn about addiction from a somewhat detached and clinical point of view, as if it were merely a topic being studied for no particular reason except for the sheer knowledge of it. Once you have finished this entire chapter, then you may piece it all together to gain a whole, better-rounded comprehension of Gomer's problem, enhancing your "book learning" with your personal life experiences.

## (1) Chemical

When I first found out that my husband was addicted to crack cocaine, I wanted to learn as much as I could about the drug and about addictions in general. Before I was with my husband, I had never spent any time around drugs or drug users, so I was totally naïve and ignorant on that score. First, I went to the local Alcoholics Anonymous meetinghouse and watched a video about addiction. That video, although helpful, didn't satisfy many of my questions. If anything, my curiosity was piqued. The video stated the addict would have cravings and irrational behavior, something I already knew firsthand, but it didn't attempt to explain why.

About a year later, one of my college courses was Biological Psychology,[1] which gave me a more in-depth understanding of what was happening chemically inside my husband's brain as a result of his drug use.

For those readers who have a background in neuropsychology, this presentation will be oversimplified; however, I am writing this assuming the reader has no previous knowledge. I am specifically keeping the terminology and processes to a bare minimum. Readers who wish to study brain chemistry in greater detail will find many books on the subject at a local library under "neuropsychology" or "chemistry of the brain."

Within the human brain there are billions of neurons, also known as brain cells, which are all carrying out processes at the same time. One brain cell tells the next brain cell to relax or to excite, to speed up activity or to slow it down. Sometimes a neuron is at rest, waiting for an impulse that

---

[1]   Textbook used for the college course and as a reference for this section: Kimble, Daniel P. *Biological Psychology*, 2nd ed. New York, Harcourt Brace, 1992.

tells it to get busy. When we sleep, for instance, many neurons are at rest, and a few others remain busy keeping us breathing and perhaps dreaming.

Drug use alters chemical transmissions from one neuron to the next within the brain of the user. The following possibilities are the primary ways in which drug use can wreak havoc on brain cells and their activities.

(a) Some drugs impersonate real brain chemicals within the brain of the user. Since the drug fits perfectly into the receptor of the next brain cell, it is fooled into accepting a false message that was never intended. This may explain why drug users are often paranoid and may have "trips" depending on the type of drugs they are using. This also explains why drug users are commonly irrational in their thinking and their behavior.

(b) Some drugs block the real brain chemicals from sending an intended message to the next brain cell. Although the drug doesn't impersonate and fool the receptor this time, it does sit in the receptor and prevent the real brain chemical from binding properly and sending its message. The receptor will neither accept nor send an intended message without the proper fit. This may explain why users' thoughts, moods, and behaviors are often erratic, why they are not mentally "with it," and why their interests often change.

(c) After a brain chemical has been sent from one brain cell to the next, the brain chemical attempts to return to be used again for another message. This process is known as reuptake. I call it the brain's recycling program. Some drugs keep the brain cells from completing reuptake, and therefore, the good brain chemical may be expelled from the body as waste. When a brain cell starts running low of any given chemical, it works hard to manufacture what it needs. However, the brain depends heavily on reuptake, and manufacturing enough brain chemicals from scratch is very slow, with brain transmissions possibly being disrupted. The result? Intended messages are not being sent from one brain cell to the next, since there are not enough brain chemicals needed to carry out the message. Long-term, hard drug use can leave a user in a seemingly permanent brain fog.

(d) Some drugs may cause brain cells to send out more of a particular chemical than is necessary. This can be harmful for a couple of reasons. First of all, too many chemicals on the receptors can distort the intended message, since it takes a particular amount of a given chemical to create any given message. Therefore, too many or too few brain chemicals, or using incorrect chemicals, distort the intended message. Secondly, the reuptake process may not be able to handle the large number of excess chemicals, thus allowing many of the chemicals to be destroyed as waste from the body.

(e) Some drugs disturb the manufacture and release of brain chemicals. When needed chemical production is slowed or stopped, brain messages will not be sent as intended. The result is the same as when a drug inhibits the brain cell from releasing its brain chemicals.

A drug may affect chemical transmissions within the brain of a user in more than one of these ways simultaneously. For instance, a drug may impersonate a real brain chemical while also inhibiting the reuptake process. Imagine the devastation to the message process! The real chemicals are sent out but cannot be used, because the drug has already bound to the receptor of the next brain cell. In addition, the real brain chemicals cannot be recycled either, so they are dissolved and removed as waste from the body. When the person stops using the drug, the receptors are left vacant, but now the real brain chemicals are all gone or severely limited in number. The brain is left crying out for what's missing. This is addiction at the chemical level.

When Gomer stops using, how long will it take for the brain to manufacture enough brain chemicals so that Gomer has a normal level available and his cravings subside? This depends on the length of drug use, the types of drugs used, and the amount of drugs used. My husband had been using a variety of drugs off and on for nearly 20 years, in great amounts at times. Marijuana, cocaine, and alcohol were his favorites. It will likely take several years of total sobriety for his brain chemistry to equalize, allowing his cravings to go away. Perhaps the manufacturing equipment in his brain has been permanently damaged so that some amount of craving will always exist (short of a miracle of God). No one can say for certain.

This broader understanding of chemical addiction helped me cope a bit better with my Gomer's cravings, withdrawals, and mood swings. I now know why it's futile to try to reason with someone high on a drug or coming down off of it. Most of all, it helped me realize the truth about addiction: to goes *far beyond* someone wanting to simply quit bad enough.

(2) Psychological

Addiction is complex, involving psychological issues in addition to the chemical aspect already discussed. Addicts have their own emotional skeletons, as we all do. You have probably figured out or even talked about some of them with your Gomer. Perhaps Gomer was abused as a child; maybe his parents divorced or some other traumatic event left a wound or scar on his emotions. That's not to say that all addicts had something tragic happen to them, but, in my experience, many of them have.

Perhaps you feel Gomer should be over it. Maybe you believe what happened in the past shouldn't have affected Gomer to the degree it did. Maybe Gomer feels the same way and denial may partially be the reason why Gomer hasn't dealt with it. Nevertheless, this line of reasoning is totally irrelevant and a waste of your time. The fact is, it *did* damage Gomer on some level, and—let's just go ahead and face it—Gomer isn't over it yet. Hoseas and Gomers both must stop arguing over what should be and start dealing with what is. The hard truth is, Gomer may have never even faced his emotional hurts. Even worse, Gomer may not ever be aware he has emotional hurts. He may believe he is already over it or convinced that he's a tough guy and was never hurt to begin with. Does this statement sound familiar to you? "I'm not the one with the problem! You're the one with the problem!" Gomer has probably said that to you with a hard, emotionless face. I know my Gomer did.

Gomer often has an extremely low self-esteem hidden under a tough exterior. This tough exterior is what Gomer built to protect his weak, emotional insides from any more harm. I think of it as a house being rebuilt after a tornado. The owner has put up extra strong outside walls and painted them so anyone going by would admire his rebuilt house. But inside! He swept the rubbish all into one room, where no one, including himself, is allowed to go. He tries to act like the tornado never happened or at least didn't bother him. No one can speak about the mess in the room. It scares him. If and when Gomer allows, you will discover his insides are a mess.

How can you help Gomer with the psychological aspect of addiction? There are things you should remember that will help you both to expose and to heal Gomer's emotional wounds of the past. When Gomer chooses to reveal his hurts, keep in mind the following:

1. **Listen**. Listen without comment when Gomer wants to talk about past or present hurts. Allow Gomer moments of silence. Sometimes Gomer will share more of his insides if we would just learn to keep quiet.

2. **Say very little**. This obviously goes hand in hand with listening. Nod your head. Touch Gomer's arm tenderly. Refrain from finishing Gomer's sentences. Help Gomer to relax by not staring at him. Be careful that you don't look shocked at anything he has to say. Don't take offense to anything either, even if you are being directly implicated in Gomer's pain. You're not there to react; you're merely a sounding board. Gomer may have never said any of this out loud to anyone before, so he is very vulnerable and fragile.

3. **Don't judge**. Our first instinct when listening is to offer advice, telling Gomer not to feel the way he does. We say things like, "You shouldn't feel that way." We talk like we have the answers: "You just need to stop thinking about it." The problem is that to Gomer our advice sounds like judgment. Maybe it shouldn't, but it does. Allow Gomer to express how he feels and what he felt without having to defend his emotions to you. Gomer needs total freedom to express. Only if Gomer asks specifically for your advice during a heart-to-heart should you give it, and even then, do so sparingly.

4. **Refrain from saying "I understand."** You don't understand, even if you are recovered yourself. Gomer's personal experiences are solely his own. Don't lace his story together with one of your own by adding, "I know all about that ..." If you have a similar story, tell that to Gomer some other time when he appears interested.

When Gomer wants to share his story, in whole or in part, revert to listening only. When you repeatedly tell Gomer you know all about it each time he talks to you, it makes Gomer not want to tell you anymore. Why should he, since you already know it all? It also can make Gomer feel inadequate or foolish knowing that you went through perhaps the same thing and you do not appear to be hurting or messed up like he is.

5. **Expect these open talks to be short, especially at first**. Don't try to prod more out of Gomer. This will make Gomer reluctant to expose himself to you again for a while, maybe permanently. You'll learn more by allowing Gomer to control the length and timing of the talks. When he changes the subject, drop it! As a Christian, pray that Christ will help Gomer to realize and deal with past/present hurts and fears. Also pray that Christ will give you the wisdom to know when to be quiet and what to say, if anything at all.

6. **Keep it quiet**. Don't divulge Gomer's inner workings to anyone who could even remotely or accidentally let him know you told his secrets. It's best to keep it completely to yourself. If you must talk with someone, choose your confidant carefully: your pastor, counselor, or a trusted Christian friend perhaps, but only if they are sympathetic toward Gomer's plight. Sharing his information with someone who feels little or no compassion for addicts will only add stress to you. They may even begin to reject you when they are not able to understand your patience with Gomer's struggles, and this may bring you down emotionally. They may also begin to look at Gomer differently. So choose carefully.

7. **Thank Gomer for sharing.** When you feel it's appropriate, remind him he can talk to you anytime he wants to, about anything. Now, drop the subject. You may be dying to know more, but pressing won't help. Gomer will talk again when ready and not until then. I sometimes wouldn't thank my husband for sharing until the next day. For instance, driving down the road seemed to be a good talking time for him. So the next day or week, when he seemed in a talking mood in the car, I would thank him for sharing with me.

9

That's about all I would say. Many times, my thank-you prodded him to open up to me again, but not every time.

8. **It's not an excuse**. Remember, whatever happened—whatever hurts Gomer is harboring inside, whatever pain Gomer experienced in the past or present—is merely an explanation of drug use, never an excuse. The fact that Gomer turned to drugs is a distinct issue. Allow Gomer to feel whatever he's feeling, but don't get caught up thinking it's okay that Gomer turned to drugs, considering what he's been through.

It will likely take a long time for Gomer's emotional wounds to heal, even once he's willing to open up. This is not because of the addiction—this is just because Gomer is human. These tips apply to anyone who has emotional issues, not just addicts. The initial process of pouring antiseptic on a festered cut is often more painful than getting cut in the first place. A severe wound often requires several bandage changes as the wound oozes. Then, even when it appears to have healed, it can still be tender. The area may always be a weak point, easily torn back open.

Allow Gomer to express feelings of hurt, anger, distrust, etc., during this antiseptic phase. Expect Gomer's emotions to ooze for a while. Help him change bandages as often as he will let you. Be careful around the hurting area so it doesn't get reinjured or reinfected. Once it appears healed, remind yourself it's still a sore spot. Don't be surprised if Gomer remains weak in that area. After all, it was once severely wounded.

## (3) Cultural

There is more to addiction than chemical and psychological issues. A third aspect is cultural. Drug use isn't the taboo it once was. Many people believe it's no big deal, even cool and expected. Then when the person's life is destroyed and he is out of control, Gomer's friends often think, "What's his problem?" They may even think more drugs or different drugs are the answer. "Man, you can't handle liquor! You need to calm down. Here, take a hit on this."

Hoseas often blame the friends, thinking, "If only those friends would leave him alone, he would be okay." Be careful. This line of thinking is dangerous! It takes the blame off Gomer and places it on others. Although they probably don't help matters any, it's not ultimately their fault or responsibility. It also stirs up your anger, which can lead to a bigger rift between you and Gomer. Gomer can tell when you resent his friends, and then Gomer resents you. The more you press Gomer to stay away from those "bad" friends, the more Gomer may want to prove that you can't tell him who he can and can't hang out with.

My husband had one or two common places to get his drugs. I found myself hating those towns and everyone in them. The fact is, drugs can be purchased on most street corners in America today, in both rural and urban neighborhoods. Drugs know no social or economic barriers. No town is exempt. Again, the blame is not on the area or the people. Gomer—and only Gomer—is to blame. He chose to make the buy. He chose to take the hit.

Most people in today's American society truly believe that you can experiment with drugs on all levels and then walk away, free and clear, when you *really* want to. Although some say they have done just that, these folks are the exception. This cultural undercurrent propels the notion that some recreational drug use is perfectly all right. They may encourage, tease, or taunt someone into participation, totally unaware they may be fueling an addiction problem.

Moreover, often Gomer is not the sole addict in the family. One member may be hiding the destruction better than Gomer is, but the addiction is still there, hiding in the shadows. Maybe it's a sister addicted to prescription Valium, or a nephew hooked on porn. Then there's the alcoholic mother or gambling father. Not all addictions involve illegal drugs.

Why do I mention this? Gomer may have inherited a strong addictive personality. Whether you believe addictive personalities are genetic or environmentally induced, other addicted family members would have direct influence on Gomer either way. Most likely, it won't be easy for Gomer to break the addiction, particularly if other close family members are using drugs too. They may not be addicted to the same degree as Gomer, so they probably won't understand why it's ruining Gomer's life; after all, using drugs isn't ruining their lives. They may be in denial about their own addiction. They may not even admit using. Nevertheless, their influence is unlikely to benefit Gomer's attempt to quit.

Drug addicts must leave behind much more than just drugs to achieve sobriety and lasting recovery. Drug use draws the user into a unique subculture with its own attitudes, beliefs, values, rules of conduct, and daily patterns. Let's take a minute to look at these cultural aspects more closely.

**Attitudes**: Our attitudes influence every aspect of our lives. A good attitude can help us through a bad day. Conversely, a bad attitude can make us want to quit during our very best day. What are the overall attitudes of drug users?

- Make good while you can.
- Just don't get caught.
- If it feels good, you might as well do it.
- Why bother trying; good won't come to me anyway.
- Life is miserable, then you die.
- Life is a party, then you die.

**Beliefs**: We all hold our own beliefs in life. We believe certain things about the nature of humankind that guide how we interact with others. We believe certain things about God that influence how we interact with him. We believe things about ourselves that impact our daily actions, too. What do addicts tend to believe about themselves and others?

- The better you treat others, the more they'll use you.
- No one really cares anyway.
- If I died right now, no one would even notice.
- This (misery) is as good as life gets.
- I've been too bad for too long to change now.
- I do drugs because I like them—I'm not addicted.
- I'm not hurting anyone else.
- I'm no good to anyone.
- I'll never amount to anything more, so why even try?

**Values**: A person's value system is responsible for setting priorities in their life. It's not hard for me to recognize, because of my values, that feeding my child takes higher priority than buying myself a new dress. It's easy for me to keep a job, because I know how important it is to keep the bills paid in order to have a roof over my head and food on the table. Addicts usually have altered value systems. What are the common values among addicts?

- Few values exist when craving or using the drug.
- Top priority goes to getting the drug, even over paying bills, caring for children, or prior commitments or any kind.
- Loyalty to other users and drug dealers is highly valued (i.e. Never squeal on them, regardless of the consequences.).

**Rules of conduct**: We all follow unwritten rules of conduct that guide how we act in situations and when we react to situations. For instance, except for addicts, most people I've known offer some form of greeting when they come for a visit and some sort of good-bye when they take their leave. This is a rule of conduct, or protocol if you will. However, addicts hold to their own set of behavioral codes. What are the unwritten rules of conduct among addicts?

- Don't ask or answer, "Who was that on the phone?"
- Don't ask or answer, "Where are you going?"
- Come and go at will, without a word.
- Talk in code so others overhearing have nothing to tell the police.
- Be constantly aware of your surroundings (almost paranoid).
- Say very little, especially over the phone.
- Mumble when you do talk (may be trying to hide the drug-ruined teeth).
- Lie for other users and drug dealers to help cover their tracks.

**Daily patterns**: Daily patterns are routines that we find ourselves in, usually out of necessity, in order to get things done. Weekday patterns may be: get up; go to work; go home; make dinner; help kids with homework; bathe; watch TV, go to bed. Weekends might be a little different: get up;

mow the yard; go to the store; clean the garage; etc. What daily patterns do addicts have?

- Few routines, if any.
- Hustling for a buck.
- Rambling to find their dealers/drug friends.
- Secretive about where they've been.
- Hard to pin down where they are going.
- Can't say for certain when they will return.

Why do you need to understand the drug subculture? So you don't unrealistically expect Gomer to rearrange his whole life in a week, a month, or even a year after he says he wants to quit. Suggest changes slowly when he seems receptive to hearing helpful suggestions. Drip honey on his belief that no one really loves him. Work on his attitude that he will never amount to anything. Encourage him regularly. Celebrate the small successes. Tell him you love him. This admission doesn't mean you like or condone his drug use; it simply means you love him. That's all. And you do love him. You must, or you wouldn't be reading this book for help. If you didn't love him, you could have walked away without a single backward glance.

When Gomer decides to quit, almost every aspect of his life—his friends, his lifestyle, his hangouts, his attitudes, his everything—must change too. It's never as simple as just quitting. As you can see, there are plenty of changes to work on just in the cultural area alone. Their life changes won't happen overnight. As an educated Hosea, don't expect them to.

## (4) Spiritual

There is a spiritual aspect to addiction. Although the words "drug" and "addict" are not found in the Bible, the destructive path of the addict is clearly described in several passages. The book of Proverbs has many allegorical references to drug addiction and alcohol. Other Biblical passages predict its course as well. When reading the listed passages in Proverbs to help your understanding, consider the words of the allegory and what they could mean. An immoral woman, evil woman, or harlot in our case is the drug or the addiction. For example Proverbs 5:3–4 (NKJV) might then mean:

> For the [enticement of drugs seems sweet and alluring] but in the end [addiction] is bitter as wormwood, sharp as a two-edged sword. [Addiction's path] goes down to death and [the ways of an addict] lay hold of hell.

Let's consider what the Scriptures say.

First, God gives a stern warning to avoid the evil pathway of life and to follow his wisdom instead. In Proverbs 1:7, 20–33 and 2:1–20, notice how at some point the person described in this passage turned away from wisdom. In Proverbs 5:1–14, 20–23, God warns again that if a person does not listen to his wisdom, a road of destruction will follow. Nevertheless, these passages also encourage those who would listen to seek his wisdom, which he gives generously so that our lives will be truly blessed.

This is again confirmed in James 1:5–8. We Hoseas *need* wisdom: wisdom to deal with Gomer; wisdom to believe or not believe; wisdom with our finances that are left in shambles; etc. Whether Gomer seeks God's wisdom or not, won't you seek it? Ask for it now, and believe Christ will give it to you.

In Proverbs 6:20–28, there are more promises of how to avoid trouble and what will happen if you choose not to listen. Ecclesiastes 7:26 (NKJV) says the person who pleases God will "escape from her," which in our case refers to escaping the chains of addiction, but the "sinner shall be trapped by her." It also says her heart is "snares and nets" and her "hands are fetters." Would anyone dispute that drugs are like chains and fetters?

Next God describes the life of those who have ignored wisdom. Proverbs 7 is a great allegory to drug use. When my husband read this for the first time, he was astonished at how accurately it depicted the road of destruction upon which he found himself with his own addiction. This passage depicts the typical story of most Gomers. Proverbs 23:26–35 continues to tell about the Gomer-lifestyle and mind-set. This Scripture makes a clear reference to the regular and abusive use of wine and alcohol.

Joel 1:1–2:27 outlines destruction too, but don't miss the keys to restoration—real repentance. God wants addicts to know that although they have allowed the consuming "locust" to waste much of their lives, God will restore them if they will but repent of their ways and turn to him. He is faithful. What is the consuming locust to an addict if not drug use itself?

Hosea 4:11 teaches us the heart can be enslaved. Anyone who has been close to an addict would readily compare them to a slave—a slave to the drug. Hosea 4:12 (NKJV) says it's a "spirit of harlotry." Harlotry in the Bible is often used as a reference to a person who sinfully and willfully turns away from God and God's ways. Romans 6:15–23 (NKJV) talks of slavery, too; we are slaves to whatever we obey. The drug addict obeys his drug cravings; therefore, the Bible calls him a slave and the drug his master.

The issue of slavery is again mentioned in 2 Peter 2:19 (NLT), which says a person is "a slave to whatever controls" him. The New King James Version uses the word "conquered." The addict is controlled by the drug. Slaves are not free to leave of their own accord. In Romans 7:14–25 Paul agrees that we are not able of our own will to ultimately control our sinful urges. In fact, we'll even do things we hate when sin controls our lives (vs. 15 and 20). It makes sense then that Gomer can detest the drugs yet still not be able to say no. Thankfully Paul tells us that although we can't control it ourselves, there is one who can deliver us from the slavery of sin—Jesus Christ (Romans 7:24–25).

Galatians 5:19–24 lists the works of the flesh. Drunkenness and the like are listed among the works of the flesh. The opposite, temperance (self-controlled), is listed with the spiritual fruits. It's no surprise then that an addict manifests many of the works of the flesh, such as outbursts of wrath, selfish ambitions, dissensions, and revelries. Should a Christian expect spiritual fruits from anyone who is not of Christ? Are those addicts who have given their hearts to Christ suddenly made perfect? Have you already arrived at perfection?

Galatians 6:7–8 (NLT) promises, "You will always harvest what you plant." Is it then possible to sow into addiction without reaping the corruption and troubles outlined throughout Scripture? God's word does not lie. It plainly states that you *will* reap what you sow. A more in-depth study of reaping what you sow comes in the next chapter of this book, entitled the Rules of Reaping.

According to Scripture, Gomers are spiritual fools. Why? Because they lack the knowledge of God. Moreover, they think they are wise on their own and do not need wisdom from on high, or anybody else for that matter. Obviously, by that definition, Gomers are not the only spiritual fools, but since this book deals with addicts, we will focus on them. As you read the following Scriptures, you will see a picture of your Gomer emerging.

In the New King James Version (NKJV) of the Bible, Proverbs is full of references to spiritual fools:

- 1:7 "fools despise wisdom and instruction"
- 1:22 "fools hate knowledge"
- 10:21 "fools die for lack of wisdom"
- 14:1 "foolish" destroys their own house
- 14:9 "fools mock at sin"
- 14:16 "a fool rages and is self-confident"
- 15:2 "the mouth of fools pours forth foolishness"
- 15:5 "fool despises his father's instruction"
- 15:14 "fools feed on foolishness"
- 15:32 a fool "despises his own soul"
- 18:6–7 "his mouth calls for blows" (he asks for it!)

Other passages in the NKJV talk about Spiritual fools:

- Psalm 53:1–3: Fools are "corrupt, and have done abominable iniquity."
- Isaiah 5:11–12: They "follow intoxicating drink."
- Isaiah 5:13–20 describes the fool's pride; they are exalted against God.
- Isaiah 5:21–24: Fools are "wise in their own eyes."

The New Living Translation (NLT) of the Bible also mentions fools:

- Luke 12:20–21: Fools "store up earthly wealth, but [do] not have a rich relationship with God."

- Jeremiah 4:22: God says "My people are foolish and do not know me."

Proverbs also uses the words "simple" and "scoffer" as descriptors. In Scripture, the term simple refers to the unwise, and scoffer refers to those who are full of pride. The following passages are all from Proverbs (NKJV):

- 1:22: Scoffers "delight in their scorning" (making fun of others).
- 13:1: "A scoffer does not listen to rebuke."
- 14:6: The scoffer "does not find wisdom."
- 14:15: "The simple believes every word."
- 14:18: "The simple inherit folly."
- 15:12: "Nor will [the scoffer] go to the wise" (to learn from them).
- 21:24: The scoffer "acts with arrogant pride."

> Woe to those who are wise in their own eyes, and prudent
> in their own sight!
> Woe to men mighty at drinking wine, Woe to men valiant
> for mixing intoxicating drink,
> (Isaiah 5:21–22 NKJV)

**Conclusion:**

When you put all these aspects together—the chemical, psychological, cultural, and spiritual—you begin to comprehend the full scope of Gomer's difficulties in quitting and why relapse is so common. Gomer may wholeheartedly desire to quit, but the chemicals in his brain are screaming for what's missing. Meanwhile, the lack of a drug high has allowed Gomer's emotional mess to rise up in him. Let's not forget the drug-friendly friends, family, and our culture in general are telling Gomer that drugs are okay; just use a little for fun and relaxation. As if these stumbling blocks aren't enough to keep Gomer off-balance, the spiritual battle for the soul is raging, though Gomer is probably completely oblivious of this.

Don't expect Gomer to even acknowledge you are being affected by his addictions. From time to time, Gomer may admit he's placed a financial hardship on you, but other than that, Gomer will be well into recovery before he can look past his own personal misery and admit to being the major cause of your distress as well. We Hoseas desperately want Gomer to acknowledge responsibility for our hurt, but that is unlikely to happen until Gomer has recovered enough to have healed within himself, at least a little. If Gomer struggles dealing with his own emotional mess, why would you think he can deal with admitting he's caused you pain, too? It's simply more than Gomer can do (anytime soon).

Understanding Gomer's struggle may help you deal with your own struggles a bit better. As much as your struggles are related, they are distinctly their own at the same time. One of the reasons I wrote this book was because I wasn't able to find anything to help *me*. All the books I found seemed to focus solely on helping Gomer, which would in turn help me, I suppose. But, what if my Gomer didn't help himself? Where was my help? I was drowning. So as I found Scripture, as I had insights and, through experience, found things that ended up working, I wrote them down. I looked them over frequently (as you will this book), because the road isn't straight—it's sometimes circular.

Be careful how you use this new understanding. It's very easy for Hoseas to get caught up in "helping." You have probably been doing all you knew to do before you found this book. If you are like I was, you have followed Gomer all the way down his path of destruction attempting to help him, but, instead, you have nearly destroyed yourself as well. The only real help for Gomer is when Gomer finds and uses God's strength together with his own strength to fight his addictive urges while making definite changes in nearly every aspect of his life.

After reading this book, you will no longer be naïve enough to believe Gomers should just be able to quit if they really want to. Now you know it's a real battle within them, a battle they may not be strong enough to win or even attempt to fight very often. The war will only be won when they *do* fight for themselves long enough and hard enough. Nevertheless, we know there are things we can do to assist them in finding that strength, because we now understand more fully the nature of addiction. In the end, though, Gomer's battle is not *your* battle. It is Gomer's battle alone.

Keep reading.

There is so much more to know.

# CHAPTER 2

# RULES OF REAPING

Do not be deceived, God is not mocked;
for whatever a man sows, that he will also reap.
(Galatians 6:7 NKJV)

This theme of consequences is written throughout God's word. The rules of gravity—what goes up must come down—apply to reaping. You *will* reap what you sow. Sow *good*—reap *good*. Sow *bad*—reap *bad*. The "rules" promise blessings when you sow "good" seeds. Those same rules promise consequences when you sow "bad" seeds. It works both ways. Consider yourself a gardener who foolishly plants green bean seeds along with weed seeds. Silly for a gardener, I know, but if you did it, you wouldn't be surprised to see both green beans and weeds coming up in the garden plot. Yet with life, we often think doing good things should take away the consequences of any bad things we've done. That is not what Scripture tells us, and life experience confirms Scripture has it right.

Allow me to use money issues as one example in this lesson. Let's say for many years I have had poor financial planning and spending habits, so that I owe money to a lot of places (I've scattered many bad seeds). Now I see the error of my way and begin to be very careful with my money. I have every intention of paying off all my many debts (I'm starting to plant good seeds now). The debts I owe are still collecting interest charges and late payment fees. My foolish spending last month before my change of heart now comes in the mail with another new bill to pay. Even though my habits and intentions have changed, the consequences of what I've done still must be dealt with. None of this is surprising, is it? The good news is over time, if I persist in doing what is right and best, the results from my old bad habits will diminish, and the results of my newer, better habits will rule the day. But this takes time, doesn't it? And this is just one example.

> Today I have given you the choice between life and death, between blessings and curses. Now I call on heaven and earth to witness the choice you make. Oh, that you would choose life, so that you and your descendants might live! (Deuteronomy 30:19 NLT)

So let's consider what the Bible actually teaches about sowing and reaping.

## 1. Timing

It's important to realize that neither the blessings nor the consequences are promised to occur when *you* think they should. Maybe you have been faithful but you don't feel blessed right now. This is when you must exercise your faith, believing God's promise of blessings will come in his perfect time. Daniel stood holy before God, yet he was put into a den of hungry lions (Daniel 6). I'm sure Daniel didn't feel blessed when that door first opened and he was shoved into the den of lions. Yet God is faithful, and Daniel was not harmed. God's promised blessings followed Daniel's faithfulness. The tenth chapter of Daniel also records a time when Daniel prayed for three full weeks as he waited for an answer to his prayer. Again, faithful perseverance will see you to blessings.

Ecclesiastes 3:4 (NLT) reminds us that there is "a time to cry and a time to laugh. A time to grieve and a time to dance." Don't give up on God's promised blessing. Remember Galatians 6:9 (NLT) says, "So, let's not get tired of doing what is good. At just the right time we will reap a harvest of blessing if we don't give up." 2 Chronicles 15:4–7 (NLT) tells us that in great times of turmoil we are to turn to God, "as for you, be strong and courageous, for your work will be rewarded!" What an awesome promise! Hold on … your time is coming. Keep doing what is right, what is best, what is godly.

## 2. The Choice is Yours

Read Deuteronomy 30:11–20. In verses 11 through 14 God tells us the rules of reaping (and more importantly, the way of salvation) are easy to understand. They are not complex or hidden or a mystery. Then he goes on in verse 19 to explain that we each have a basic choice to make. Either we will choose life (eternity in heaven) and blessing in life by loving God through faithful service to him (living life in a way that is pleasing to him—doing things his way), or we choose death (eternity in hell) and curses in our life now, through our disobedience to his word (living a life displeasing to God—not doing things his way). He wants us all to choose the better way, but he has given us freedom to choose. He is not a spiteful, vengeful God; nevertheless, he is consistent with what he promises. He gave us this choice.

You may be thinking, "I would never choose to be cursed!" True enough, but by simply *not* choosing to walk in his blessings by doing things that please him, you have chosen the curses by default. If I asked you to go with me to the movies and you ignored my request, you would choose not to go by default. It's either or. In this life, we each choose what we want to do. So, based on your choices, sit back and watch the results show up in your life. Don't be mad at God. Instead, choose differently. It's not too late to choose the blessings after all. That's the good news Jesus brought!

## 3. Kinds of Consequences

So, what kinds of consequences should we expect? Let's back up to Deuteronomy 28. This entire chapter outlines what you can expect from choosing his blessings (vs. 1–14) or from choosing his cursing (vs. 15–68). Notice in Deuteronomy 28:2 and in the latter part of 28:15 that you cannot prevent them from happening. It says, "They will come upon you and overtake you" (NKJV). It's just a matter of time. If you choose the blessings, they overtake you. You can't stop them (and really, why would you?). If you choose the cursing, they overtake you. You can't stop them (even though you might try).

If you choose his blessings, he promises health and happiness here on earth. You will be fulfilled and at peace. Of course Deuteronomy 28:1

stipulates that you must be diligent and careful to obey him in all things in order to reap this blanket of blessings. Verses 15 through 68 reverse these blessings into curses on your health, the health of your family, your wealth, and your overall happiness. In other words, you will be miserable and empty, both emotionally and physically.

## 4. More Details Please

Deuteronomy 10:12–22 simplifies what it means to be diligent and careful. The very essence of Christian servitude is described here. Verse 12 tells us to walk in His ways. It's very common today to see people wearing the abbreviation WWJD on an accessory or item of clothing. It stands for "What Would Jesus Do." We must go beyond knowing what Jesus would do. We must actually start doing what Jesus would have us do. We are ambassadors for Jesus on this earth. The entire blessing and cursing theme is written again in Deuteronomy 11:13–28.

God has warned his people repeatedly throughout the ages and throughout his word about the dangers of choosing to serve any god other than God Almighty himself. Exodus 23:20–33 promises his protection and prosperity if the people do not fail to serve him. He reminds us again in Leviticus 26:3–13 that he longs to bless us, but we must serve him with our whole hearts and souls.

In Deuteronomy 28:14–45, he reminds us in vivid detail of the destruction that we will suffer as we (mankind) choose to turn away from him. I feel I must stress to you that personal destruction can take on different forms. A person may be filthy rich, living in a mansion, and traveling all over the world but, at the same time, be utterly empty inside knowing and feeling his life is without meaning.

You need to recognize that God is perfectly capable of blessing you for your faithfulness while Gomer is harvesting a wild crop of thorns. Your blessings are not based on Gomer's actions. You cannot lose your blessings just because Gomer acts badly. Consider the words of God:

> Therefore thus says the Lord GOD: "Behold, My servants shall eat, But you shall be hungry; Behold, My servants shall drink, But you shall be thirsty; Behold, My servants

23

shall rejoice, But you shall be ashamed. (Isaiah 65:13 NKJV)

It may appear to you that Gomer isn't reaping what he has sown. Maybe it looks like Gomer is having a good time while you are suffering. Read 1 Timothy 5:24–25. His time is coming, especially when the enablers around him stop enabling. Consider also Deuteronomy 29:19–20:

> And so it may not happen, when he hears the words of this curse, that he blesses himself in his heart, saying, "I shall have peace, even though I follow the dictates of my heart"—as though the drunkard could be included with the sober. The LORD would not spare him; for then the anger of the LORD and His jealousy would burn against that man, and every curse that is written in this book would settle on him, and the LORD would blot out his name from under heaven. (Deuteronomy 29:19–20 NKJV)

Regardless of when the consequences begin—when Gomer (or any person) turns from his evil ways, he still has some consequences to face from the bad seed he has sown. The Israelites learned this the hard way just like most of us still do. One such example is written in Numbers 13 and 14, when they refused to enter the land of Canaan, which God had promised them. Their refusal to trust God angered him. Their distrust was sin before the Lord. Although the Lord forgave them of this sin in Numbers 14:20, God still meted out the consequences in Numbers 14:22–38.

You can't expect someone who has done drugs any length of time, destroyed his credit, has no money and has a bad work history, to immediately find a great job, have money to spare/save, and have no trouble dealing with his drug cravings the very day, week or year he starts to clean up. These problems, to name a few, are the promised consequences that Gomer will have to face and deal with. And although God promises restoration (and his word does not lie), he did not promise instantaneous restoration. That will come with time as Gomer becomes more and more faithful to God's ways with much perseverance.

There are many Scriptures concerning the rules of reaping. The ones already discussed in this chapter as well as others are listed below. This list is not exhaustive. You can find more in the Bible when you begin to look for them. As you study, notice that God has been very clear. He has never tried to hide the facts from us. He wanted us to know what to expect from our actions and choices. He is not a hateful, vengeful God. He declared the rules ages ago and put the consequences into motion. We simply have made our choices, and we often make bad choices, don't we?

Check off the Scriptures below as you study them. Many of the Old Testament Scriptures talk about obeying the Jewish laws of Moses. The point of reading these particular Scriptures is to understand how God is merciful (forgiving for a time as we learn from his correction) and yet still there comes a time of judgment for rebelling against God. The consequences are not intended to drive us away from him. Hear what God is saying. The consequences are meant to drive you straight back into his arms, his love, his forgiveness, and his ways of doing things. He saw we needed a savior to intercede for us, and he sent Jesus Christ to do just that—a sacrifice for our sins. Even with this forgiveness, these Scriptures teach us how consequences come to us in this lifetime.

- Exodus 23:20–33
- Leviticus 26:3–45
- Deuteronomy 10:12–22
- Deuteronomy 11:26–28
- Deuteronomy 12:28
- Deuteronomy 29:19
- Deuteronomy 30:11–20
- Judges 10:10–16
- 1 Samuel 12:20–25
- Job 4:8–9
- Psalm 89:30–34
- Psalm 109:17–19
- Proverbs 1:30–33
- Proverbs 22:8
- Isaiah 1:16–20
- Isaiah 57:15–21

- Jeremiah 2:13–35
- Jeremiah 17:5–11
- Lamentations 3:27–40
- Hosea 8:7
- Hosea 10:12–13
- 2 Corinthians 9:6–11
- Galatians 6:7–9
- 2 Peter 2:4–11

# CHAPTER 3

# COMMUNICATION GUIDELINES

> You cannot separate fools from their foolishness, even
> though you grind them like grain with mortar and pestle.
> (Proverbs 27:22 NLT)

I know exactly what it's like trying to talk to Gomer, trying to reason with him so he will understand the destruction he is causing, and trying to get him to assume responsibility for it. I know what the goal of my "talks" were, too—I wanted to see a light bulb come on behind his eyes and immediately see him change back into the person with whom I had first fallen in love. I often thought, "If I could just break through to him!"

God gave us basic instructions on how and when to communicate with Gomer. No—really, he did! This chapter will outline those communication guidelines for you and give you the scriptural passages that underlie them. Just because Gomer comes in ranting and raving doesn't mean you have to yell and scream back at him. When Gomer shouts and curses at you for no good reason (is there a good reason?), you don't have to defend yourself or try to explain your actions to him.

Once I started following these principles, my own frustration level dropped way down, nearly out of sight. I understood why I couldn't "break through" to my Gomer. I realized why certain times were better than others to start talking about the problems. I found strength in God to walk away from an argument and to avoid starting a fight (even when I really wanted to yell and scream at him!).

Someone said to me once (after her Gomer had a bad run in with the person he was getting his drugs from), "Do you think he has learned his lesson?" You see, that Hosea still didn't understand herself that addiction recovery isn't about a Gomer learning enough lessons to be able to quit. She remained frustrated—daily ranting, raving, quarreling, and preaching to her Gomer (her grandson).

The following six rules for communicating with Gomer will take conscious effort on your part. They will not be easy, nor will they come naturally to you. And don't think for a minute that Gomer will play by these rules or will be interested in these rules, so don't expect him to. Don't even bother telling him you are following "rules." These rules are for *you*. These rules are to help you keep your own sanity and prevent you from wasting your time, energy, and vocal cords. Stop fighting with Gomer. Apply the rules.

**Rule #1**
**Don't try to reason with Gomer.**
**Addiction isn't logical.**
**You cannot reason them into sobriety.**

As you found out in chapter 1, addiction involves many things, but wisdom and logic are not among them. The Lord considers a person foolish who refuses God's wisdom, counsel, and authority. Casting good judgment aside, Gomer has taken a wrong path. Once far enough along that path, brains cannot guide him back. He cannot find his way out using logic, no matter how smart he is. This is not about being dumb. This is addiction. You can be very intelligent yet foolish. You can be a genius yet be personally destructive. Consider the following Scriptures and what they teach you about communicating with your Gomer.

> On the lips of him who has understanding, wisdom is found, but a rod is for the back of him who lacks sense. The wise lay up knowledge, but the mouth of a fool brings ruin near. (Proverbs 10:13–14 ESV)

The way of a fool is right in his own eyes, but a wise man listens to advice. (Proverbs 12:15 ESV)

There is a way that seems right to a man, but its end is the way of death. (Proverbs 14:12; 16:25 NKJV)

The tongue of the wise uses knowledge rightly, but the mouth of fools pours forth foolishness. (Proverbs 15:2 NKJV)

Every way of a man is right in his own eyes, but the Lord weighs the hearts. (Proverbs 21:2 ESV)

Wisdom is too lofty for fools. Among leaders at the city gate, they have nothing to say. (Proverbs 24:7 NLT)

You cannot separate fools from their foolishness, even though you grind them like grain with mortar and pestle. (Proverbs 27:22 NLT)

Trying to reason with Gomer, especially while Gomer is under the influence of his drugs, is futile. You are wasting your breath. You are merely frustrating yourself. That's all. You're not breaking through or making headway. Really, you're not. Gomer either agrees with you, because he knows that you're right (even though that's not enough to stop the addiction) or because he hears your words as harping at him or lecturing him, and he doesn't want to hear it. Agreeing seems the quickest way to shut you up. If he disagrees, it's just a heated, ugly fight. Fighting is never productive. Either way, logic isn't going to break the addictive pattern.

There will of course be times, perhaps, when Gomer seems more receptive to talking about the drug problem. This is the only time reasoning with Gomer may prove effective or lead to recovery. Typically Gomer is well into his recovery before you can truthfully have meaningful conversations about what he has been doing.

**Rule #2**
**Don't try to correct or instruct Gomer.**
**They know deep inside they should do better; they just can't or are not ready to stop.**

How has Gomer reacted to your instructions so far? Does the Bible describe it well or not? Telling him what he should be doing, how he should live his life, etc. is another waste of your time. Obviously, if your Gomer is under eighteen parental guidance is needful and appropriate. But even in this case you will discover the Scriptures prove accurate. It's especially true when your Gomer is an adult.

It's sad to watch a person with so much potential and ability waste years chasing after a drug. I remember telling my husband, "You're a big boy, do what you wanna do." I was tired of the hassle, trying to get him to do differently. I figured out he was going to do whatever he wanted to do (and he did), so why should I exhaust myself attempting to block the path. I also think my saying that started pouring into him the idea that he truly was "choosing" to do the drug; that he could "choose" not to; that options actually did exist.

Consider the Scriptures below.

> So don't bother correcting mockers; they will only hate you. But correct the wise, and they will love you. Instruct the wise, and they will be even wiser. Teach the righteous, and they will learn even more. Fear of the Lord is the foundation of wisdom. Knowledge of the Holy One results in good judgment. Wisdom will multiply your days and add years to your life. If you become wise, you will be the one to benefit. If you scorn wisdom, you will be the one to suffer. (Proverbs 9:8–12 NLT)

> A single rebuke does more for a person of understanding than a hundred lashes on the back of a fool. (Proverbs 17:10 NLT)

Don't answer the foolish arguments of fools, or you will become as foolish as they are. (Proverbs 26:4 NLT)

As a dog returns to its vomit, so a fool repeats his foolishness. (Proverbs 26:11 NLT)

Do not give what is holy to the dogs; nor cast your pearls before swine, lest they trample them under their feet, and turn and tear you in pieces. (Matthew 7:6 NKJV)

No one puts a piece of unshrunk cloth on an old garment, for the patch pulls away from the garment and the tear is made worse. Nor do they put new wine into old wineskins, or else the wineskins break, the wine is spilled and the wineskins are ruined. But they put new wine into new wineskins and both are preserved. (Matthew 9:16–17 NKJV)

In the multitude of words sin is not lacking, but he who restrains his lips is wise. (Proverbs 10:19 NKJV)

## Rule #3
## Stop arguing and fighting with Gomer.

Fighting only causes more damage. Discuss problems with Gomer only when he is receptive, even though that might not be very often. If a fight or argument ensues, then drop the subject for the time being. Pray. Do what you must do. Make the right decision without Gomer's approval or input as necessary. But stop fighting about things. Arguing solves nothing. Below are Scriptures for you to glean from.

Hatred stirs up strife but love covers all sins. (Proverbs 10:12 NKJV)

Starting a quarrel is like opening a floodgate, so stop before a dispute breaks out. (Proverbs 17:14 NLT)

It is honorable for a man to stop striving, since any fool can start a quarrel. (Proverbs 20:3 NKJV)

The north wind brings forth rain and a backbiting tongue an angry countenance. (Proverbs 25:23 NKJV)

A stone is heavy and sand is weighty, but a fool's wrath is heavier than both of them. (Proverbs 27:3 NKJV)

If a wise man contends with a foolish man, whether the fool rages or laughs, there is no peace. (Proverbs 29:9 NKJV)

For as the churning of milk produces butter, And wringing the nose produces blood, So the forcing of wrath produces strife. (Proverbs 30:33 NKJV)

If it is possible, so far as it depends on you, live peaceably with all. (Romans 12:18 ESV)

But avoid foolish and ignorant disputes, knowing that they generate strife. And a servant of the Lord must not quarrel but be gentle to all, able to teach, patient, in humility correcting those who are in opposition, if God perhaps will grant them repentance so that they may know the truth, and that they may come to their senses and escape the snare of the devil, having been taken captive by him to do his will. (2 Timothy 2:23–26 NKJV)

Even so the tongue is a little member and boasts great things. See how great a forest a little fire kindles! And the tongue is a fire, a world of iniquity ... Out of the same mouth proceed blessing and cursing. My brethren, these things ought not to be so ... but the wisdom that is from above is first pure, then peaceable, gentle, willing to yield, full of mercy and good fruits, without partiality and without hypocrisy. Now the fruit of righteousness is sown in peace by those who make peace. (James 3:5–6, 10, 17–18 NKJV)

**Rule #4**
**Use few words.**

Speak calmly. Choose your words wisely. Avoid saying the same things over and over. Does this rule apply to Gomer? No, of course Gomer is probably running at the mouth, cursing, and saying the worst. You, however, should remain in control of your own mouth. Say it once. Say it twice if needed. Yes, speak calmly and with finality. That's enough. It's been said. Repeating it doesn't make it truer. Then do what you said you'd do—or is Gomer like a spoiled child that gets his way so long as he keeps whining and aggravating you? Are you that easy a target? Should you be?

A soft answer turns away wrath, but a harsh word stirs up anger. (Proverbs 15:1 NKJV)

He who has knowledge spares his words, and a man of understanding is of a calm spirit. Even a fool is counted wise when he holds his peace; when he shuts his lips, he is considered perceptive. (Proverbs 17:27–28 NKJV)

Don't waste your breath on fools, for they will despise the wisest advice. (Proverbs 23:9 NLT)

The Lord God has given Me the tongue of the learned, that I should know how to speak a word in season to him who is weary. He awakens me morning by morning, He awakens my ear to learn as the learned. (Isaiah 50:4 NKJV)

Live wisely among those who are not believers, and make the most of every opportunity. Let your conversation be gracious and attractive so that you will have the right response for everyone. (Colossians 4:5–6 NLT)

So then, my beloved brethren, let every man be swift to hear, slow to speak, slow to wrath; for the wrath of man does not produce the righteousness of God. (James 1:19–20 NKJV)

## Rule #5
**Don't expect or demand rational thoughts or actions from Gomer.**

Although at times they may appear logical and in control of themselves, their overall pattern will prove irrational and quite unpredictable, even well into recovery. Don't let any of this surprise you. Remember these rules are about your own sanity and expectations. Think about it; much of life's frustrations and anger stem from faulty expectations. We expect to check out quickly at Wal-Mart; this faulty expectation breeds frustration and anger on our part when the line moves slowly. On the other hand, when we get in line at Wal-Mart fully expecting to wait, we are more able to handle this wait with grace and patience, even humor. We expect to make the drive to work in fifteen minutes, but a traffic jam causes the commute to be forty-five minutes. What if when we left the house we fully expected that the drive would take up to an hour? Wouldn't we be able to handle it better? These are merely two examples. Have faulty expectations been driving your emotions all over the place?

Apply this same reasoning to your expectations with Gomer. What should your expectations be? When Gomer surprises you with good decisions and actions, then you can be pleased, of course. In the meantime, keep your expectations in line. This rule isn't about thinking negatively or having little faith in God's willingness and ability to bring change in Gomer. It is about being real with yourself about where Gomer is *today*. Find balance on this long, bumpy road.

Folly is joy to him who is destitute of discernment, but a man of understanding walks uprightly. (Proverbs 15:21 NKJV)

Excellent speech is not becoming a fool, much less lying lips to a prince. (Proverbs 17:7 NKJV)

Let a man meet a bear robbed of her cubs, rather than a fool in his folly. (Proverbs 17:12 NKJV)

Putting confidence in an unreliable person in times of trouble is like chewing with a broken tooth or walking on a lame foot. (Proverbs 25:19 NLT)

## Rule #6
## Avoid playing games.

Avoid playing "I'll show him!" or "If he can do it, so can I" games. Be honest with yourself. You don't really want to do the same things that Gomer does. You don't want to behave unreliably and irresponsibly. Also, it destroys all your credibility when you do get to talk to Gomer. All Gomer has to say is, "You do that, too!" Preserve your own dignity; do not lower yourself to Gomer's standards; wait on the rules of reaping to kick in. Then, when Gomer is willing to listen to what you have to say, you can say it in the pureness of your heart. Consider the words of the Lord:

Don't say, "I will get even for this wrong." Wait for the Lord to handle the matter. (Proverbs 20:22 NLT)

Do not say, "I will do to him just as he has done to me; I will render to the man according to his work." (Proverbs 24:29 NKJV)

Then Jesus called to the crowd to come and hear. "Listen," he said, "and try to understand..." "Don't you understand yet?" Jesus asked. "Anything you eat passes through the stomach and then goes into the sewer. But the words you speak come from the heart—that's what defiles you. For from the heart come evil thoughts, murder, adultery, all sexual immorality, theft, lying, and slander. These are what defile you. Eating with unwashed hands will never defile you." (Matthew 15:10, 16–20 NLT)

Bless those who persecute you; bless and do not curse. Repay no one evil for evil. Have regard for good things in the sight of all men. If it is possible, as much as depends on you, live peaceably with all men. Beloved, do not avenge yourselves, but rather give place to wrath; for it is written, "Vengeance is Mine, I will repay," says the Lord. Therefore "If your enemy is hungry, feed him; If he is thirsty, give him a drink; For in so doing you will heap coals of fire on his head." Do not be overcome by evil, but overcome evil with good. (Romans 12:14, 17–21 NKJV)

A righteous man who falters before the wicked is like a murky spring and a polluted well. (Proverbs 25:26 NKJV)

Do not envy the oppressor, and choose none of his ways. (Proverbs 3:31 NKJV)

Do you not know that in a race all the runners run, but only one receives the prize? So run that you may obtain it. Every athlete exercises self-control in all things. They do it to receive a perishable wreath, but we an imperishable. So I do not run aimlessly; I do not box as one beating the air. But I discipline my body and keep it under control, lest after preaching to others I myself should be disqualified. (1 Corinthians 9:24–27 ESV)

# PART TWO

# PIECING YOU BACK TOGETHER ... AND OVERCOMING!

## CHAPTER 4

# DON'T CLAIM THE BLAME

Where did all your feelings of guilt and blame come from? There are three distinct possibilities: *You* blame you; *Gomer* blames you; or *others* blame you.

You need to come to a full realization that Gomer's addiction is *not* about *you*. Gomer has a need to blame people and circumstances other than himself for his messed-up life: if the kids behaved better; if finances were better; if he had a more rewarding job; if his parents were still together; if the kids at school didn't bully him. The list goes on and on. Fill in the blank yourself: if money was good or bad; if his job was great or awful; etc. Either way, the drug would still be a priority. Are you ready for reality? It's called addiction, pure and simple. Now that Gomer has a craving for the substance, that drug calls Gomer's name, no matter the circumstances.

Do you blame yourself for Gomer's addiction? Perhaps you have low self-esteem and believe you are so boring that Gomer would rather get high with friends than spend quality time with the likes of you. I speak from experience. These were many of my own feelings. If only you were prettier, smarter, more interesting, sexier, etc. You're possibly convinced that at least some of it must be your fault.

Does Gomer blame you, saying you drove him to the drugs? If you didn't nag so much; if you worked more; if you worked less; if you were somehow different, then he wouldn't do drugs. If Gomer is your child, he too may say things to you or to others that imply it's your fault, such as, "You're too old-fashioned; you don't care about him anyway; you expect too much from him," etc. Once again, the blame is being wrongfully placed on your shoulders.

Do others, such as Gomer's family or friends, say things to place the weight of the burden on you? If you didn't work nights, then Gomer wouldn't be so lonely. That's why he does drugs. Or, if you showed him you really loved him, then he wouldn't be so messed up.

Whether you, Gomer, or others place the blame on you, the results are the same: you have an enormous weight on your shoulders that you didn't create. You may believe you are left without the power to do anything about it. Well, get your highlighter out! Here's the good news! First of all, you didn't cause the addiction, unless of course you held Gomer down and forced him to consume the drug until addiction took hold. I'm assuming you didn't do that, so Gomer needs to take personal responsibility for the addiction, and you need to let go of that blame. After all, we all have blows in life (Ecclesiastes 3:11–12 NKJV). Each person deals with problems individually. Not all people turn to drugs, and we all must learn to be constructive in how we handle life's difficulties.

> But let each one test his own work, and then his reason to
> boast will be in himself alone and not in his neighbor. For
> each will have to bear his own load. (Galatians 6:4–5 ESV)

Gomer's need to blame others is really a defense mechanism so he doesn't have to face his own personal weaknesses. The Bible says these weaknesses stem from our sinful nature—so we all have them—however, Gomer generally does a really poor job facing them. To read about this in the Bible, see Luke 5:8; Matthew 9:4; Romans 3:23; Genesis 6:5; Numbers 32:14, and Isaiah 1:4–6. I'm sure these are not the only verses you could list here.

You may recall from chapter 1 that perhaps Gomer had a bad experience in life—something that opened him up to experiment with drugs to begin with—nevertheless, the drug caused the addiction, not you. Gomer made a poor choice and allowed his body to experience the drug. Gomer must assume full responsibility for making the initial choice to try the drug. Even if you were partying with him and encouraged him to try it, let's say you even tried it with him, it was still ultimately *his* choice to do it with you. You are not to blame. Gomer made that choice.

That's not to say you were perfect either. Maybe you could have been a better spouse or parent or sibling or friend. Maybe there's truth in that—you could or should have done things differently. Regardless, the addiction is still not your fault. Again, each person makes his or her own choices. Gomer made a bad choice when he chose to escape his troubles and pain with drugs instead of a healthier method. He could have sought out a counselor at school, talked to the pastor at a local church, called a neighbor, or asked another relative for help. Drugs were not his only option. Stop feeling guilty. Stop feeling ashamed. Stop claiming the blame. Read Philippians 3:12–16.

Let's go deeper. There are many ways we Hoseas claim the blame. For instance, have you ever changed your plans based on what Gomer was doing? Perhaps you'd better not go to the store now, because if you're not home, Gomer might slip off and use. Or what about all those times you didn't make plans at all, because you sat by the phone at home, hoping he'd call so you could convince him to come home? You are taking on the burden of whether he uses or not, as if his drug use is a sole result of what you do or don't do. That's claiming blame! Recognize it for what it is and stop it! Gomer's drug use is a direct result of Gomer's personal choices, not *your* choices. Nothing you do or don't do will keep Gomer sober and clean. Let's face it: if it were up to you, Gomer would already be clean and living a joyous, prosperous life. So tell me again, how is this *your* fault?

Let's go even further. Now that you realize you have been claiming the blame, I'm going to assume you don't want to claim the blame anymore. How do you stop? How do you put the responsibility back on Gomer?

I want you to think of as many statements as you possibly can that Gomer has made that make you feel guilty or somehow responsible for his addiction and actions. Regardless of whether or not you think you should have felt guilty, write these statements down in the space provided below or on a separate sheet of paper. Write down whatever you can think of now.

As days and weeks go by, when you hear Gomer or others say things that make you feel guilty or responsible for his actions, come back to this paper and write them down, too. Maybe it's, "If you had come straight home …" or "If you didn't nag …." You know what Gomer and others say to you. This list is *not* being made to show Gomer. This isn't about showing Gomer what he's doing to you. In fact, except for showing it to a counselor who may be helping you through all this, I would keep this list private and hidden away. This list is for you. It's all about *you* learning more about *you*—how *you* are wounded and how *you* can be healed on the inside.

Start listening for those toxic statements, and write them down. It's important that you learn to recognize what is causing you to feel the weight of guilt. Gomer and others may not be aware that these toxic statements are placing guilt on your shoulders, but you need to become aware of them in order to deflect them effectively.

Example #1: "You're so stupid! I'm out of here! I need to relax!"

Example #2: "You work all the time. No wonder I hang out at (drug friend)'s house!"

1.

2.

3.

4.

5.

6.

7.

8.

9.

10.

Next, I want you to learn to deflect this guilt. When I say *deflect*, I mean you don't feel guilty to begin with; you don't take on the guilt at all. Say the following statement out loud to yourself: "I'm sorry you feel that way." Go ahead. Really. Say it out loud. Say it again. From this point forward, whenever Gomer (or anyone else) makes statements to you that assign responsibility to you for Gomer's drug problems, I want you to say that statement either out loud or to yourself. "I'm sorry you feel that way." Resist the urge to argue. Don't attempt to defend your past actions. Simply say, "I'm sorry you feel that way." This statement is a powerful way to redirect the misguided feelings you have so readily taken on in the past. Start using it as your only defense.

I'm not giving you carte blanche to knowingly or purposefully do or say things to push Gomer's buttons. On the other hand, you can't be tormented by Gomer's every emotional whim. Drug addicts are prone to emotional roller coasters—out-of-control one minute, sweet and loving the next. Allow Gomer his own feelings, like anger or depression, without feeling the same emotions yourself. Refuse to take part. Ignore his ranting as often as possible. This will get easier with practice. Simply say, "I'm sorry you feel that way."

This really worked for me. This simple response, nothing added, broke the stronghold of guilt off of me somehow. I started out saying it sarcastically, or angrily even, to my husband and others. Over a couple of months, the sarcasm and anger faded away, and I found I meant what I was saying. I really was sorry they felt that way. I saw how pitiful it was for them to think any of this mess stemmed from my behavior, how truly pitiful that they really couldn't face the truth of the matter; how absurd it was to go through life thinking their mess was caused by others. So the anger and sarcasm became unnecessary. I meant what I was saying in all honesty and with love from my heart. I knew I couldn't change anything.

My husband's reaction to this statement was varied. Sometimes he tried to poke at me, to lead me into a fight. I had to remain strong. I would repeat the statement, "I'm sorry you feel that way." Nothing more. There was really nothing to add. Unless he was willing to face his mess, my words were a waste of time at that point. I had said everything anyway, so many times. I was tired. I was glad to say nothing more. Sometimes he would walk away, especially after I had done this for a while. But above all, over time his statements of blame occurred less frequently. I wonder if my deflecting that guilt landed the guilt squarely back on him, and he felt it somehow (without really understanding even), so he threw guilt my way less and less?

As one example, I used this statement the day I moved out. The truth of his addiction had been out for a while. He refused help. He refused to acknowledge anything much. We were facing life without electricity and water. There was very little food. I realized I could use my small paycheck at the time to pay the electric bill but then have no money for gas or food— or I could move out until he got his act more together, if ever. I chose to move out. I came home and began to quietly pack when he asked me what I was doing. I told him. He was *not* impressed with my decision. But no matter what he said, my *only* response was, "I'm sorry you feel that way." Sounds crazy, but it felt so good not to argue back. I knew I was making a good decision, so I couldn't allow his emotions to change my course. He said, "Well, what am I supposed to do without electricity?" I shrugged and said, "I'm sorry you feel that way." He threatened to kill himself. I said, "I'm sorry you feel that way." He swore he'd never speak to me again. I said, "I'm sorry you feel that way." He claimed I'd better take everything I wanted, because he would throw it all in the yard and burn it when I left. I said, "I'm sorry you feel that way."

This story is not exaggerated. About the only other thing I said that day was, "Here's the number where you can reach me. I'm not thinking divorce, but I won't live like this anymore." He screamed at me, "I'm not calling you!" Again, I shrugged and said, "I'm sorry you feel that way." I left. Of course he called. Of course he tried using every angle to get me back without having to face the truth. I think you know what I said to him. "I'm sorry you feel that way."

Galatians 5:1 tells us to not be entangled again with the yoke of bondage. Paul was actually talking about the bondage of religious ceremonial practices, but what better way to describe Gomer's emotional mess than a "yoke of bondage." In Jeremiah 2:19-21 God explains his willingness to break our bonds if we would only be willing to live for him. Learn, and be willing to trade in the yoke of bondage for what Christ has to offer you.

Is this not the fast that I have chosen: to loose the bonds of wickedness, to undo the heavy burdens, to let the oppressed go free, and that you break every yoke? ... The Lord will guide you continually, and satisfy your soul in drought and strengthen your bones; you shall be like a watered garden and like a spring of water whose waters do not fail. (Isaiah 58:6, 11 NKJV)

Come to Me, all you who labor and are heavy laden, and I will give you rest. Take My yoke upon you and learn from Me for I am gentle and lowly in heart and you will find rest for your souls. For My yoke is easy and My burden is light. (Matthew 11:28–30 NKJV)

For you will break the yoke of their slavery and lift the heavy burden from their shoulders. (Isaiah 9:4a NLT)

It shall come to pass in that day that his burden will be taken away from your shoulder and his yoke from your neck and the yoke will be destroyed because of the anointing oil. (Isaiah 10:27 NKJV)

Remember, you too are allowed your own distinct emotions. You may be upbeat and cheery when Gomer is angry or discouraged. Learn to console Gomer without sinking emotionally yourself. You do it with others, like your neighbor or friend. Perhaps they lost a job or a relative died. You talk with them, but when you are finished talking with them, you're still fine. You still sleep at night. You still get hungry and eat a normal meal. You still keep your plans to go shopping or to read. Do the same with Gomer. How does it help if you fall into the same emotional pit as Gomer? Conversely, Gomer may be on top of the world while you had a perfectly rotten day. That's okay, too. Don't expect Gomer to take on or understand your emotions either. Empathy is nice but not something Gomers are typically able to show or feel until well into recovery.

Addiction is very much an emotional problem. It's emotions, both good and bad, that Gomers haven't learned to deal with. They use drugs to forget, to escape, and to celebrate. Anger comes easily. They pretend to be fearless when really they are full of fear. Regardless of the emotion, Gomer doesn't know what to do with it. Gomer is so used to the artificial feeling of numbness from drugs that any real emotion is foreign to him. Emotions have long been covered up under the blanket of drugs. See Ephesians 4:17–19 (especially verse 19).

From my own experience and from talking with many other Hoseas, I've determined that Hoseas tend to be hyper-emotional, taking on the emotions that Gomer casts off. We feel their emotions for them. For example, the threat of a police warrant for his arrest should disturb Gomer the most. But Gomer seems undisturbed by it, continuing as Gomer normally does—drugging, hustling, lying, etc. Meanwhile, it's Hosea who takes on seemingly extra worry for Gomer. Hosea spends extra effort trying to fix Gomer's problem so Gomer won't be in trouble; reminding Gomer repeatedly about the fine he needs to pay; trying to wake Gomer up in time to go to court; and trying to get Gomer to deal with and fix his own problems. Hosea loses sleep and appetite spinning mental wheels while trying to think of some way to fix Gomer's predicament. These are Gomer's problems, so let Gomer handle them, or let him face the consequences. Yes, this can be hard to do, but it needs to be done.

This is the emotional trap we Hoseas find ourselves in when we claim the blame. When you learn to deflect these unearned millstones of guilt that hang from your neck with chains of embarrassment, you will discover a whole new power to improve your life—a new surge of energy and determination will rise up in you that you didn't know existed.

If, however, after reading this book you still feel guilty for Gomer's addiction, then I suggest you seek professional Christian counseling. Satan loves to keep God's people beaten down with past guilt and mistakes. Christ is all about forgiveness. If you have asked for God's forgiveness, then learn to accept it. It's there freely for the taking. God remembers it no more. When others remind you of your past mistakes or try to pin blame on you that should rest on someone else, what do you say in reply? "I'm sorry you feel that way." (Very good! You're learning!)

The following Scriptures will help you find and personally accept Christ's forgiveness for you, too:

- 2 Chronicles 30:9
- Proverbs 1:29–33
- Isaiah 55:7
- Jeremiah 31:34
- 2 Corinthians 5:17
- 1 John 1:5–10
- Isaiah 38:17
- John 3:16–21
- Matthew 9:1–8
- Luke 7:36–50
- Romans 5:1–11

# CHAPTER 5

# STOP ENABLING

E nabling. What does it mean?
Enabling means doing or saying things that allow or make it easier for an addict to continue using.

Do you do it?

Most Hoseas believe they are *not* enablers. After all, they plead with Gomer to stop. They cry and pray for Gomer to stop using. They run after Gomer whenever needed to help Gomer leave his drug lifestyle and friends. They give Gomer a place to stay each time Gomer says he is ready to get clean.

What many Hoseas don't understand is that *most* helping *is* enabling. Drug use is disastrous. To think you can do things that can magically make drug use cease without Gomer ever facing his mess full-on is simply not reality. Let the cards fall where they may, no matter how bad it will be for your Gomer. Don't protect Gomer anymore from the inevitable repercussions of his drug use. Why should Gomer ever face the real results of his actions so long as someone else works to cover up his dirty reality? Gomer says, "What mess?" If there are few or no consequences, why does Gomer need to stop?

So you still don't believe you are an enabler? Let's list some common ways that we Hoseas enable our Gomers:

- Paying Gomer's bills when you know the money was spent on drugs.

- Lying to others and yourself that Gomer's just struggling keeping a job, or was laid off, etc.
- Cooking a special or favorite meal as soon as Gomer comes home, because you know he's not been eating right while he's been out on a drug binge. (Proverbs 19:10, 15)
- Giving or loaning money to Gomer when he says he needs it for gas, etc. He says he'll pay it back soon. Of course, he never has paid back the money from last week or the week before.
- Bailing Gomer out of jail.
- Paying Gomer's fines so he doesn't go to jail to begin with.
- Co-signing for loans. (Proverbs 22:26–27)
- Not sticking to what you say you'll do. For instance, you told Gomer last week that it was the last time you'd give him gas money, but you gave him more today anyway. (Matthew 5:37)
- Displaying your own emotional extremes toward Gomer. One minute you're raging mad. The next minute you're codling him with pity. (Galatians 5:22–23)
- Putting up with Gomer's drug friends or activities because you're afraid saying no would make Gomer mad or leave. (Proverbs 13:20; 24:1–4)
- Allowing or tolerating the use of lesser drugs (alcohol or marijuana) in your house in the hopes that at least Gomer will stay at home and off the harder stuff. (Ephesians 5:1–11)
- Not reporting physical abuse. You're afraid Gomer will face trouble, or you're afraid of Gomer. You may simply be embarrassed to admit you've been abused.
- Lying to others to cover up Gomers' drug activities. For instance, saying Gomer was home sick when you know Gomer skipped school or work.
- Doing everything Gomer wants in the hopes that keeping him happy will keep him clean.

So how many things on the list have you done at least once? Realizing that you have been enabling still doesn't make the addiction your fault. Don't go back to claiming the blame. It just means you've been making it easier for Gomer to continue. The choice to use is always his to make.

Honestly evaluate the things you do that enable Gomer so you can make a conscious effort to stop doing those things. As you evaluate your actions, you may come up with things to add to my list above.

How will Gomer react to these changes? Oh! He's *not* going to like them one bit! You should also be aware that Gomer is likely to be very angry when you stop enabling him. He likes things to go his way. He likes knowing he can always get more money from you. He likes knowing you'll cover for him. What should you say to his begging? How should you reply to his angry outbursts of cursing you to your face? "I'm sorry you feel that way." Don't bother explaining. They really *know* why. Deep inside, they *know* why already. Just calmly offer the pitiful phrase, "I'm sorry you feel that way."

There are two big reasons you *must* stop enabling.

(1) You are only fueling the addiction with all its habits and lifestyle.
(2) You are keeping yourself burdened down. Take back control of your life and your finances! Openly stating the truth about your life (no matter how messed up it is) and actually doing just what you said you'd do is *very* empowering. You will feel relief!

Am I saying then that Gomer should *never* be given any help at all? Of course not! Everyone deserves a break. We all need a helping hand from time to time. But this "help" should be very little and rare, and only when Gomer asks for it while showing serious effort to change. Otherwise the "help" is merely enabling Gomer to continue drugs without having to face the real consequences of what he's doing.

Once you realize which of your actions have been enabling Gomer, don't do those things anymore. Stop yourself. If you continue to enable, don't be angry at Gomer when he uses the "gas money" to run around instead of looking for a job. Instead, get mad at yourself, and learn from it. Promise yourself that you won't do it again the next time you have the chance. Build some backbone by saying that strange word, "No!"

For instance, Gomer asked you for money to fix his car. You wanted to say no, but instead you gave him your last hundred dollars. You find out a couple days later that he blew the money, and his car is still not fixed—it's not even being worked on. Now you are strapped for cash and could really use that hundred dollars for groceries. You get angry at Gomer. You should be angry with yourself instead. You *knew* he had addiction problems. You *knew* he has blown nearly every dollar you have given to him in recent months. *You* took the chance. You *could* have said no. You *should* have said no.

I want you to realize from this you have every right to say no. It's *your* money, *your* home, *your* car, *your* food, *your* everything. You are hereby released from spending your last dime on Gomer. You are released from dropping everything you are doing at the drop of a hat just because Gomer calls requesting something. You are released from running to rescue Gomer from his mess. You are released!

Now is a good time to mention what I call "the circuit." A circuit is made up of many enablers. I promise, you are not the only one enabling Gomer. There are other relatives, friends, churches, etc. all willing, from time to time, to offer Gomer "help." This is crucial to understand, because you may be thinking, "But I only help Gomer a couple times a year." This may be true of each enabler in Gomer's circuit. When you finally say no, Gomer simply has to find someone else in the circuit that will say yes.

Gomer often pits the enablers against one another, too. Maybe Gomer told you how he's struggling right now, because Uncle Gary didn't pay him yet for the work Gomer did on Uncle Gary's house. This breaks down your resolve to say no, and it sounds legit (Uncle Gary is cheap, after all), so you say yes to helping Gomer out this time. Had you taken the time to follow up on Gomer's claim, Uncle Gary would have told you how Gomer lived over his garage for two months and never looked for a job or helped out. Then Gomer promised to fix the leak in the roof, which he never did, but he took the money for supplies, and Uncle Gary hasn't seen him since! Multiply this con to a dozen different enablers who are living far enough apart or may not even know each other, change the con to fit what each enabler might fall for, breed distrust between all the enablers, and voila! You have a working circuit!

When you stop enabling, you can't make everyone else in the circuit stop. You may not even know who all the other enablers are. You could try to talk with the ones you know, share the ideas from this book, but they may or may not believe Gomer is "that bad." All you can do is your best to break your piece of the circuit as much as you can. The rest you must walk away from. A good way is to follow up on each of Gomer's stories. "But Gomer will think I don't trust him." So? Excuse my sarcasm, but if Gomer's so trustworthy, why are you reading this book? There is only one way to know if Gomer's stories are true. Make the calls. Be discreet if you wish. If you were wrong in your mistrust, then apologize. But from my experience, your mistrust will prove right at least 90 percent of the time. Pray for God himself to change the minds of other enablers, for the truth to be revealed to them. Finally, remember what you already know—the choice to use drugs is always Gomer's choice. You can only do what *you* can do.

There is no cure. Once he becomes an addict—cocaine, alcohol, or gambling, etc.—there is no way of knowing for sure whether or not Gomer will ever completely escape its cruel web. Nevertheless, Gomer is more likely to face the grim reality of his addiction when the Hoseas in his life stop enabling his habits. The ultimate decision to change still rests with Gomer, but the best way to help him stop using is to stop enabling. And then, too, either way, you will have peace in your daily living.

# CHAPTER 6

# FINANCIAL ACCOUNTABILITY

As soon as you know money is being spent on drugs, you must begin to protect yourself financially. Today is not too late to start. You are responsible for planning and controlling your own personal income. If you are not currently working and are solely depending on Gomer to provide for the financial needs of the household, then it is time for you to come off the bench and step up to the plate. If you don't make every effort to do what you are capable of to earn a living for yourself, then you are at least partly to blame if you are living in poverty.

You must do what you can to earn an income to pay for basic needs, such as rent or mortgage, electricity, gas, and food. If Gomer does pay a bill, that's great, but addiction eventually may take its toll, and you may find yourself in a real financial mess (if you haven't already) unless you take some action. If you are not physically able to work, have children at home, or if you haven't worked in years, then pray that God will provide you with some way of earning an income, and look for work within your abilities. Don't just say, "I can't." After you pray, put feet to your prayers. Look through the papers, get online, and ask friends and neighbors if they know of any job openings. If you would like to babysit in your home or tend to other people's gardens, clean houses, or whatever, then post a flyer at the grocery store or anywhere you are allowed. Spread the word through friends, at church, and on social media. The idea is to do everything possible, then rest in God's promise of provision.

If you are working and you still have no money to pay the bills, because you gave some or all of it to Gomer that is your own fault and something you must stop doing. Learn to take financial control and say no to Gomer. The following is a list of suggestions for overcoming your financial woes due to Gomer's drug habits.

- ☐ Say no when Gomer asks for your hard-earned money. Even if you are convinced you should "help" this one time by paying a bill, still do not give Gomer the money. Go with Gomer to pay the bill or mail the check yourself.
- ☐ Create a secret stash of money that Gomer doesn't know about, no matter how small. Any is better than none. If you are not working, you may be able to tuck away small amounts by taking ten or twenty dollars from the grocery money without it being noticed. Make an agreement with yourself that this money is only for real emergencies. Plan on being able to pay the monthly bills and normal everyday expenditures without dipping into the fund as much as possible.
- ☐ Cut back on spending wherever you can. Put the savings into your secret stash if you are able.
- ☐ Get bills out of your name as much as possible.
- ☐ Do not cosign for any more of Gomer's loans.
- ☐ Open a safety deposit box for all the car titles that have your name on them. Otherwise, Gomer can take the car title to a check-cashing or pawn shop and get money off the car title. If he doesn't pay it back, you can lose the vehicle.
- ☐ Separate your joint bank accounts. If Gomer won't take his name off the joint accounts, then take your name off of them. If he bounces checks, you are responsible along with him as long as your name is still on the account. Start your own checking account in your own name. Use a different bank. When your personal checks arrive, place the extra checks into your safety deposit box. No more joint accounts.
- ☐ Get your name off the joint credit cards, too. No more joint credit cards!
- ☐ If you own property together with Gomer, make sure your name is on the deed. You shouldn't simply take Gomer's word for it. Check it out at the Registry of Deeds office. If your name isn't on

it, Gomer can legally sell it without your knowledge, and he may never give you any money from the sale. And where do you think the money will go?

- ☐ Choose not to argue or fight over money with Gomer. Control your own income, and pay for what you must or what you honestly believe is your fair share.
- ☐ Be careful to keep your purse, wallet, checkbook, and credit/debit cards under your control and out of sight at home. Don't leave them exposed for easy access without your knowledge.

Remember, you don't have to live in poverty. If Gomer chooses to waste all or most of his money on drugs, you are not automatically his banker. Say no. Gomer won't be happy about this change in his cash flow. Saying no is not easy. He's used to you being an easy, quick pick. If it makes you feel any better, give him money *one last time* while making it very clear this is the *last time* he will get money from you. Then, when Gomer wants money again next week or next month, you can remind him that you gave for the last time, and you meant it. Don't say it unless you mean it. When you mean it, be prepared to face Gomer's unhappiness. Remember what you should say when Gomer's unhappy that you said no? "I'm sorry you feel that way."

But he says he's out of gas? Needs money? Oh, that's too bad. Car broke down? The check bounced? He needs to pay a speeding ticket, or he'll go to jail? These are all good reasons to ask someone for money; however, you and I both know that if he hadn't bought drugs and was working instead, he would have had the money. Gomer may just be lying to get the money. It's not always obvious.

When you say no, you don't need to explain or justify it to Gomer. The answer is simply no. When you stop giving cash, Gomer will ask to borrow money with the promise of paying you back soon—always soon. When you stop loaning Gomer money, then he will ask you to pay a bill for him, just this one time. Initially, you must refrain from all forms of financial contributions. Later on, when Gomer is recovering, you may deem it okay to help out occasionally, but even then, do this rarely and only while he is making a good faith effort at recovery. It is best for you both to become financially independent. Stop the borrowing cycle. Don't spend more than you earn. Go without extras for a time in order to get yourself back on track. Don't allow Gomer to waste your hard-earned income for you.

Spiritually speaking, if you are a follower of Christ, you are also financially accountable. What many Christians today don't seem to grasp is that God requires 10 percent of our increase (income or profit). In return, he promises financial blessing.

> Will a man rob God? Yet you have robbed Me! But you say, "In what way have we robbed You?" In tithes and offerings. You are cursed with a curse, for you have robbed Me, even this whole nation. Bring all the tithes into the storehouse that there may be food in MY house, and try me now in this, says the LORD of hosts, if I will not open for you the windows of heaven and pour out for you such blessing that there will not be room enough to receive it. And I will rebuke the devourer for your sakes, so that he will not destroy the fruit of your ground, nor shall the vine fail to bear fruit for you in the field, says the Lord of Hosts. (Malachi 3:8–11 NKJV)

Don't miss out on the promise of blessings! Tithes, along with all forms of Christian giving, must be done with a willing, cheerful attitude, a heart of thanksgiving and trust. Read Matthew 6:25–34 (especially verse 33). You can't out-give God. Gladly give God his part, and he will see to it you are not without what you need. Then, when God blesses you, don't hand it over to Gomer to waste; don't waste it yourself!

> The point is this: whoever sows sparingly will also reap sparingly, and whoever sows bountifully will also reap bountifully. Each one must give as he has decided in his heart, not reluctantly or under compulsion, for God loves a cheerful giver. And God is able to make all grace abound to you, so that having all sufficiency in all things at all times, you may abound in every good work. As it is written, "He has distributed freely, he has

given to the poor; his righteousness endures forever." He who supplies seed to the sower and bread for food will supply and multiply your seed for sowing and increase the harvest of your righteousness. You will be enriched in every way to be generous in every way which through us will produce thanksgiving to God. (2 Corinthians 9:6–11 ESV)

# CHAPTER 7

# OVERCOMING LONELINESS AND LOW SELF-ESTEEM

It is the Lord who goes before you. He will be with you; he will not leave you or forsake you. Do not fear or be dismayed." (Deuteronomy 31:8 ESV)

During my husband's addiction, my most difficult emotional struggle was loneliness. To be fair, before I even met my husband, I had struggled for years with low self-esteem and loneliness. Nevertheless, I had never felt more alone, more unwanted, more unlovable, or more undone than when his addiction was at its worst. During several periods of time, my husband and I only owned one vehicle, so when he stayed gone on a binge, I was left without transportation. Although I knew people to call for rides to church and to the store, I still felt isolated and pathetic. I thought I was a burden on everyone else. I was claiming the blame during this period, too, which didn't help anything at all.

My family was scattered across the country, and they didn't know about the problem for the first year or so. Once they knew the truth, I felt they were either judgmental or condescending toward me. They probably didn't mean to be, and perhaps I misunderstood, but these were my feelings. They couldn't understand or ever tolerate how I could stay with him. After that, we generally avoided the topic. My family rarely asked about Lonnie, afraid of striking a landmine of emotions and unsure of what to say in response. Friends were similar; however, they seemed a bit more willing to listen. I even knew others at the church's AA meetings whose spouses were struggling with addiction, and I attended Al-Anon for a short while. Yet loneliness was a tremendous—nearly crippling—problem for me.

How did I get through it? I had to make changes, but even the changes didn't erase my loneliness overnight. Let's list some suggested changes you could make that will help you fight the loneliness. Remember, loneliness is your own problem for which you must find a solution. Gomer is not your solution for loneliness any more than you are Gomer's solution for addiction. Gomer is not the core reason you feel lonely, either. Loneliness comes from a deeper part of you. It comes from a lack of self-esteem and isolation from others.

Both low self-esteem and isolation can be "treated" in similar ways. The first step must come from inside yourself. You must determine that you don't want to feel that way anymore and decide you will do what it takes to get over it. I know this sounds rather blunt, but it is what worked for me. That is all I know to share.

Begin by thinking about the things you *can* do. Refuse to dwell on things you *cannot* do so well. For instance, maybe you're a great cook, but you can't sing a note. Well, don't worry about the fact that you can't sing. Remember, lots of people can't sing! Concentrate on the fact that you *can* cook. Now put your ability to use. Perhaps your church cooks meals for the homeless and shut-ins. Involve yourself in this ministry. If your church doesn't do that, then talk to your pastor about starting it up yourself, or volunteer at a homeless shelter in town to cook for them. The point is this—God gave you a talent. Figure out a way to put that talent to God's use.

How will cooking a meal help your self-esteem and isolation problems? It's amazing what a difference getting involved will make! You will have something to occupy your alone time. You will be doing something you enjoy and are good at. God will bless you for working in his ministry. You will spend less time alone. You will be making a difference in someone else's life, which will make you feel good at the end of the day. Your brain will be filled with thoughts of your plans for growing your ministry rather than always thinking about Gomer and your problems.

When you get involved, you need to remember a couple of things. Everybody has opinions, and that's all they are—opinions. It won't take long before somebody says something to you or about you that could easily offend you and make you want to quit. Satan would like nothing better. In one fell swoop, God would lose a worker, and you would be isolated and lonely again. Do you think Satan will not buffet you? Determine within yourself now that the opinions of others will not sway you from God's business. They are only opinions.

Ever since I've put aside depression, I've been amazed to realize that people will ignore the opinions of others when they are positive comments and completely take to heart every opinion that is negative. This very thing happened at the church I was attending while I was writing this book. A woman sang a special song to the glory of God. She was so nervous, but as she sang it with all her might, the congregation was blessed by her willingness to obey God. Many people told her after service how they enjoyed her song and were truly blessed by it. But one person told her that she couldn't sing and that person was embarrassed for her. This woman was so hurt that she didn't return to church for a long time. Granted, that was a very ugly, mean-spirited thing that was said to her. However, she could have realized that it was only *one opinion*. Certainly, the many positive comments should have helped her see the insignificance of this one opinion, but she forgot them or chose to ignore them.

Christians must also remember that the church house is full of all kinds of people. Some are doing their best to walk with Jesus; many are not. Some go to church out of a great love of the Lord; others attend out of habit or from a false sense of eternal security. Even among the true Christians, there are different levels of maturity. Some may have gone to church their entire lives but have barely grown in the Lord (remaining babes in Christ). Others may have been saved only a short time but are hungry for God's word and have grown quickly mature in Christ.

The comments of others, which attempt to destroy your fragile self-esteem, can be handled the way as you have learned to deflect the blame for Gomer's addiction. Simply say, "I'm sorry you feel that way." Then keep on keeping on with God. You don't have to explain what you did or try to make others understand why you did it. If, however what they said is right, and you would grow as a Christian by following their advice, then put it to use without being hurt by it. If, on the other hand, the comment was simply critical or judgmental or just plain wrong, then ignore it. It's only one opinion!

I think about it this way: all comments need to get filtered through my brain. I let my brain decide which comments will help me change for the better, and I attempt to put them to use. The comments that serve no purpose except to hurt and destroy are disregarded as rubbish. God knows how fragile our human hearts are, so he gives us his peace as a guard to our hearts (Philippians 4:7); therefore, only the comments that give me joy, peace, and hope are allowed through the gates of my heart where my self-esteem lives.

The following bulleted points are suggestions for getting involved and helping you to feel better about *you*. Isolation is your choice. Choose to be active and involved with other people. You have much to offer others, and they have much to offer you. Really!

> Start making plans to get out and do things, alone or with others. For example:
> > Tennis
> > Walking
> > Jogging
> > Shopping (or just window shopping)
> Find a new hobby. For example:
> > Writing
> > Knitting or crocheting
> > Painting
> > Ceramics
> > Learning a musical instrument
> Start a project. For example:
> > Refinishing a chest of drawers
> > Wallpapering the hallway
> > Cleaning out closets for a garage sale
> Accept invitations from others. Don't sit home alone needlessly. For example:
> > Meeting for lunch

Joining a small group at church

Going shopping (you don't have to buy anything)

➤ Be honest with those who are concerned about you. When people ask you, "How are you doing?" or "Are you all right?" tell them the truth. If you are hurting and lonely, say so. Receive their love, their hugs, and their compassion. Soak it up like a dry sponge so later on, when you are home and alone, you can draw from it, reminding yourself you are loved.

➤ Volunteer to help at church. Become a Sunday school teacher or helper, clean the church, paint, plant flowers, or ask what you could do. There is always productive work to be done in God's house and in community centers, such as the Salvation Army, Meals on Wheels, Big Brother or Big Sister Programs, etc. You can volunteer at or visit the local hospital or nursing homes.

➤ Remind yourself that being alone doesn't mean you must feel lonely. There are plenty of single people out there who live happy, productive lives in spite of living alone. Talk with some happy single people you know. Ask them what they do to keep loneliness at bay.

➤ Attend church every time there's a meeting. Even though you won't always feel like going, especially alone, you will be glad you went. Go and get involved in the service rather than just sitting there thinking, "Woe is me."

➤ Learn to talk about things other than Gomer's addiction. The addiction can only consume as much of your life as you allow. The more things you are involved in, the more topics you will have for conversation, and the more others will enjoy talking with you.

➤ Talk and think about the good things you have going on in your life more than the bad things or the things you don't have.

➤ Visit the sick and homebound from church. Probably someone you know at church is in the hospital or recovering at home. Go visit that person and offer to help around the house. Cook a meal that person would like, vacuum, or do their dishes. Few things can make you feel as good as putting your woes aside to help someone else. Can't visit in person? Then make phone calls or send special notes by mail, email, text, and social media outlets.

➤ Realize that this low point in your life won't last forever, and take charge to ensure it won't.

➤ Spend time with upbeat people. The last thing you need is to hang around those who are discouraged themselves. Misery may like company, but only if you want to stay miserable! You all need to encourage each other. Skip the pity party. Seriously!

➤ Practice good posture. This may sound strange to you, but try it! Stand up straight with your shoulders back and down, head held up. You'll be amazed at how your posture affects your attitudes and perspectives. Do a double-check: stand up against a straight wall. If your shoulder blades and the back of your head touch the wall with your normal stance, then you are not slouching. However, if you must adjust your stance to make your shoulder blades and the back of your head touch the wall at the same time, then you are definitely slouching forward. This slouch could be habitual or from something such as scoliosis or osteoporosis. If you've had a habit of slouching over for any length of time, you may experience discomfort or headaches at first from standing up straight. You may find it helpful to visit a chiropractor to alleviate the pain and stiffness. Standing up straight will feel awkward at first, like you're puffing out your chest too much, but I promise it doesn't look that way to others. You don't look weird. Ask others if you don't believe me.

➤ Allow only a very small amount of time each day for crying and self-pity. It's only natural to cry and relieve emotional pressures, but allowing ourselves to give over to too much self-pity is destructive. The longer you allow yourself to stay in the pity mode, the harder it will be to come out of it. Learn to control it. Say to yourself after a good cry, "Okay, I've cried long enough today. It's time to get active." Then get up and get going.

➤ When you watch television, remember it's only TV. Real-life expectations cannot be based on what we see on TV. Their problems are resolved in thirty minutes to an hour. They are hardly realistic, nor should they be. Even so-called reality shows are planned and largely scripted. Take television for what it is—entertainment, a short-term escape from reality. Be careful not to fill all your time with it, and don't expect your life to mirror anything happening on TV.

➤ Clean the house. Lonely or depressed people tend to let the house go. They stop cleaning. Maybe because they think it doesn't matter—after all, no one comes to visit anyway. Don't fall into this trap. The clutter and filth feed your depression just like oxygen fuels a fire. Forget everybody else! Clean the house for you! And who knows? Now that you are getting more active, someone may drop by.

➤ Open the windows and let the sunshine in! Give sunshine a try! Rather than sitting in your living room with the shades drawn, get up, open the shades all the way, and bask in the warm rays.

➤ Get plenty of exercise. People who feel lonely tend to sit around. Make yourself get up and get active. Exercise causes natural chemicals to be released in your brain. So, pop in the exercise video. Take a brisk walk. Take a dance class. Buy a bicycle and start peddling. Exercise is good for your body and for your soul!

➤ Do not ignore the scriptural helps for loneliness. Look up these favorites of mine. Read them slowly and savor their words. Add your own favorite passages at the end of my list. Look at them regularly, even daily if you want to. Post them on the refrigerator, on the car dash, etc. Satan wants you to think you are all alone, that nobody, not even God, cares about you. You must remember that Satan is the father of lies. God's word is truth. Choose to think about the words of God rather than the lies of Satan.

Then you shall call and the Lord will answer; You shall cry and He will say, "Here I am." (Isaiah 58:9a NKJV)

What's more, I am with you, and I will protect you wherever you go. One day I will bring you back to this land. I will not leave you until I have finished giving you everything I have promised you." (Genesis 28:15 NLT)

And I will ask the Father, and he will give you another Helper, to be with you forever, even the Spirit of truth, whom the world cannot receive, because it neither sees him nor known him. You know him, for he dwells with you and will be in you. I will not leave you as orphans; I will come to you. (John 14:16–18 ESV)

For you are the temple of the living God. As God has said, "I will dwell in them and walk among them. I will be their God and they shall be My people." (2 Corinthians 6:16b NKJV)

See, I am sending an angel before you to protect you on your journey and lead you safely to the place I have prepared for you. (Exodus 23:20 NLT)

But I am poor and needy; Yet the Lord thinks upon me. You are my help and my deliverer; do not delay, O my God. (Psalm 40:17 NKJV)

You are my hiding place; You shall preserve me from trouble; You shall surround me with songs of deliverance. Selah. (Psalm 32:7 NKJV)

Be angry and sin not. Meditate within your heart on your bed and be still. (Psalm 4:4 NKJV)

Even if my father and mother abandon me, the Lord will hold me close. (Psalm 27:10 NLT)

At first I didn't comprehend specifically what Jesus had done to heal my depression, yet I was no longer depressed. I still occasionally fight it off like everyone else, but the dark black sucking hole no longer pulled on me. I had overcome! I pondered this miracle for years. Recently Jesus revealed to me in his word what power had healed me. I found Colossians 2:8–10 as a revelation to my spirit:

Beware lest anyone cheat you through philosophy and empty deceit, according to the tradition of men, according

to the basic principles of the world and not according to
Christ. For in Him dwells all the fullness of the Godhead
bodily; and you are complete in Him, who is the head of
all principality and power. (Colossians 2:8–10 NKJV)

Did you catch it? I didn't either at first, but let me help you find it too:
You are complete in him. That's it! With Christ living inside of me, I lack
nothing! I'm not missing anything! I'm not deficient! I'm not "retarded"
as my sisters teased me when I was young. Perhaps they were jesting, but I
had taken it in. I'm not "good for nothing," as my father so often said! I'm
not stupid, ugly, untalented, or any other negative description I've heard on
this earth. I had allowed myself over the years to be cheated through the
words and thoughts of people! But it wasn't true! I'm none of those empty
things! I am complete in Christ!

If I lack anything, I simply must ask (John 16:24). I rest in him. I
don't need approval or acceptance from *anyone* else. Christ, the God of the
universe, my creator who is the head of all principality and power, loves me
like I am and chose to live in me! He is patiently changing me to reflect
his character of love, patience, kindness, forgiveness, etc. He fills me with
his joy and his peace that doesn't waver or cower in the circumstances of
life. He holds me in the palm of his hands—those nail-pierced hands! *I
am complete!*

Grasp hold of this for yourself. If you haven't accepted Christ, I beg
you to wait no longer! He is standing at the door of your heart knocking.
Let him in. Now grab hold of the complete work of Christ in you! I wish
I were with you in person now as you read this to know that you get this,
to see the light of this truth shine in your eyes!

# CHAPTER 8

# RECLAIMING JOY AND PEACE

Thus says the Lord, your Redeemer, The Holy One of Israel: "I am the Lord your God, who teaches you to profit, who leads you by the way you should go. Oh, that you had heeded My commandments! Then your peace would have been like a river, And your righteousness like the waves of the sea. (Isaiah 48:17–18 NKJV)

When exactly did your peace of mind and happiness take leave? How do you get them back, especially in the midst of such turmoil? The apostle Paul wrote something that really caught my eye while I was preparing to speak at a woman's prayer breakfast.

And the peace of God, which surpasses all understanding, will guard your hearts and minds through Christ Jesus. (Philippians 4:7 NKJV)

He will give me his peace—a peace so strong that no one, including me, will be able to understand how I could possibly be at peace. That's what I needed! That's what I wanted! So I read a bit further.

What you have learned and received and heard and seen in me—practice these things, and the God of peace will be with you. (Philippians 4:9 ESV)

Apparently, there were things that Paul had taught the Philippian church, which he did himself, that caused the God of peace to dwell in him. What were they? Paul starts telling us back in verse four how to find and how to hold on to God's perfect peace of mind throughout life, regardless of life's bitter journeys.

## 1. Rejoice in the Lord

> Rejoice in the Lord always. Again I will say, rejoice!
> (Philippians 4:4 NKJV)

Notice Paul didn't say rejoice in your circumstances. Good times come and go. If you base your rejoicing on the circumstances, then your joy will come and go as well. Rejoice in the Lord, for the Lord is good and worthy to be praised. Period. That is why you rejoice, why you are joyful. That is reason enough to worship God. When I trust fully in God to keep his promises to me, I am able to rejoice even in the hard times.

I fear that too many Christians today do not know how to worship. It's more than just singing a song. It goes far beyond sticking a fake smile on your face so others will think you are happy worshipping God. True worship comes from the heart. It's deep gratitude and love for what God has done mixed with deep reverence for who he is—the God of all creation, the everlasting Father who loved you enough to send his only son, Jesus, as your redeeming sacrifice before God.

> Even though the fig trees have no blossoms, and there are no grapes on the vines; even though the olive crop fails, and the fields lie empty and barren; even though the flocks die in the fields, and the cattle barns are empty, yet I will rejoice in the Lord! I will be joyful in my salvation! The Sovereign Lord is my strength! He makes me as surefooted as a deer, able to tread upon the heights. (Habakkuk 3:17–19 NLT)

That is one of my favorite verses concerning the worship of God. It conveys the attitude of worship. It says that I won't always feel like worshipping. Times will be hard, but I will choose to worship God for his goodness, salvation, and help in spite of my circumstances. When you worship, you long to commune with God. You're not asking for anything, for you are too much in awe that he, the creator of the whole universe, would choose to spend time with you, and his presence overwhelms you.[2]

> You will show me the path of life; in Your presence is fullness of joy; at Your right hand are pleasures forevermore. (Psalm 16:11 NKJV)

> Honor the Lord for the glory of his name. Worship the Lord in the splendor of his holiness. The Lord gives his people strength. The Lord blesses them with peace. (Psalm 29:2, 11 NLT)

> When I consider Your heavens, the work of Your fingers, the moon and the stars, which You have ordained, what is man that You are mindful of him, and the son of man that You visit him? (Psalm 8:3–4 NKJV)

## 2. Strengthen the Inner Man (Attitude)

> For this reason I bow my knees to the Father of our Lord Jesus Christ, from whom the whole family in heaven and earth is named, that He would grant you, according to the riches of His glory, to be strengthened with might through His spirit in the inner man, that Christ may dwell in your hearts through faith; that you, being rooted and grounded in love, may be able to comprehend with all the saints what is the width and length and depth and height—to know the love of Christ which passes knowledge; that you may be filled with all the fullness of God. (Ephesians 3:14–19 (NKJV)

---

[2] For a more in-depth study of worship, I highly recommend the following resource: Tenney, Tommy, *God's Favorite House,* Expanded edition, Destiny Image Publishers, 2005.

This passage, which was also written by Paul, says to strengthen the inner man with might by his spirit. What is the inner man? I think of this as our attitude, our resolve. We must learn to strengthen our attitudes with God's spirit. This will allow us to stand in the midst of a storm and worship God. When your attitude is strong, Ephesians 3:19 (NKJV) says that you will be "filled with all the fullness of God." Is it possible to be filled with God's fullness and yet lack peace? I don't believe so. Paul spoke of his own attitude:

> But I determined this within myself that I would not come again to you in sorrow. For if I make you sorrowful, then who is he who makes me glad, but the one who is made sorrowful by me? And I wrote this very thing to you, lest, when I came, I should have sorrow over those from whom I ought to have joy, having confidence in you all that my joy is the joy of you all. (2 Corinthians 2:1–3 NKJV)

In other words, Paul had a little talk with himself. He said he "determined this with myself." Nobody talked with him. He dug deep within himself and decided not to be sorrowful anymore! Jesus, himself, testified to the need to work on our own attitudes:

> Salt is good, but if the salt loses its flavor, how will you season it? Have salt in yourselves, and have peace with one another. (Mark 9:50 NKJV)

Attitude is a choice! When you get up in the morning you can decide to be happy (rain or shine), or you can decide to be sorrowful (rain or shine). Once again, the circumstances don't determine your attitude. You choose your attitude. Choose carefully; it will affect your entire day, week, and year! Your attitude affects the decisions you make. Your attitude greatly influences where you go, what you do, and with whom you spend time.

Paul is also saying in 2 Corinthians 2:1–3 that attitudes are contagious. Don't we know it! Have you ever spent time around a person who was so unhappy (even on a good day) that before you knew it, your own good mood was flying out the window? Conversely, you've probably spent time with those who are cheerful (even on a bad day) and found yourself smiling regardless of the events of the day. Is that all there is to it? Just decide to be happy? No. It's not that simple or easy. Keep reading.

### 3. Show Kindness to Others

> Let your gentleness be known to all men. The Lord is at hand. (Philippians 4:5 NKJV)

Paul continues now in Philippians 4:5, telling us to be kind to others. Which of the following would make you feel better? Being kind to another human being and making that person's day or letting off your own steam at someone else's expense? If you chose the latter, then fall to your knees and repent. Although there may be times when it seems to make you feel better, that good feeling doesn't last. If you chose the first part, you chose well. Being kind to others, even when they don't deserve it in your opinion, creates the good feeling that truly lasts.

How you treat others throughout your day can directly impact how you feel about yourself and how close you feel to God. When you feel good about yourself as a human being who obeys God's commandments, peace and joy can enter in. They cannot dwell in an angry, bitter, unyielding vessel.

> You have neither part nor portion in this matter for your heart is not right in the sight of God. Repent therefore of this your wickedness, and pray God if perhaps the thought of your heart may be forgiven you. For I see that you are poisoned by bitterness and bound by iniquity. (Acts 8:21–23 NKJV)

> When a man's ways please the Lord, He makes even his enemies to be at peace with him. (Proverbs 16:7 NKJV)

> Who is wise and understanding among you? Let him show by good conduct that his works are done in the meekness of wisdom. But if you have bitter envy and self-seeking

in your hearts, do not boast and lie against the truth. This wisdom does not descend from above but is earthly, sensual, demonic. For where envy and self-seeking exist, confusion and every evil thing are there. But the wisdom that is from above is first pure, then peaceable, gentle, willing to yield, full of mercy and good fruits, without partiality and without hypocrisy. (James 3:13–17 NKJV)

## 4. Don't Worry or Fret

Be anxious for nothing, but in everything by prayer and supplication, with thanksgiving, let your requests be made known to God; and the peace of God, which surpasses all understanding, will guard your hearts and minds through Christ Jesus. (Philippians 4:6–7 NKJV)

Philippians 4:6 reveals another key to peace of mind. It says simply to not be anxious or disturbed for any reason. That's a hard pill to swallow, but Paul tells us what to do instead of worrying and fretting. He says to pray about it. Okay. "God help me!" No. You don't get it. Paul says to pray and to supplicate. Supplicate is an old-fashioned word. According to Merriam-Webster's online dictionary, the word means "to ask humbly and earnestly." Synonyms for this word include beg, plead, petition, implore, and beseech. In other words, if you want to release God's peace within your heart and soul, the quick "God help me" prayer won't cut it. A more earnest prayer is in order. In today's language, Paul might say, "Be passionate about your prayer."

Paul adds one more characteristic of the prayer that yields peace: thanksgiving. When you pray, thank the Lord for answering your prayer. God inhabits the praises of his people and when he inhabits us in his fullness, his peace comes with him. Have faith in God, and learn to display your faith by speaking gratitude toward God, even while waiting for the prayer to be answered. A former pastor of mine would say, "Your credit is good with me, God." In other words, the answer to my prayer hasn't come yet, but I know God heard me, and I know the answer is on the way.

Therefore I say to you, do not worry about your life, what you will eat or what you will drink; nor about your body, what you will put on. Is not life more than food and the body more than clothing? Look at the birds of the air, for they neither sow nor reap nor gather into barns; yet your heavenly Father feeds them. Are you not of more value than they? Which of you by worrying can add one cubit to his stature? So why do you worry about clothing? Consider the lilies of the field, how they grow: they neither toil nor spin; and yet I say to you that even Solomon in all his glory was not arrayed like one of these. Now if God so clothes the grass of the field, which today is, and tomorrow is thrown into the oven, will He not much more clothe you, O you of little faith? Therefore do not worry, saying, "What shall we eat?" or "What shall we drink?" or "What shall we wear?" For after all these things the Gentiles seek. For your heavenly Father knows that you need all these things. But seek first the kingdom of God and His righteousness, and all these things shall be added to you. Therefore do not worry about tomorrow, for tomorrow will worry about its own things. Sufficient for the day is its own trouble. (Matthew 6:25–34 NKJV)

Peace I leave with you, My peace I give to you; not as the world gives do I give to you. Let not your hearts be troubled, neither let it be afraid. (John 14:27 NKJV)

Until now you have asked nothing in My name. Ask, and you will receive that your joy may be full. (John 16:24 NKJV)

## 5. Change the Diet of Your Mind

Put on then, as God's chosen ones, holy and beloved, compassionate hearts, kindness, humility, meekness, and patience, bearing with one another and, if one has a complaint against another, forgiving each other; as the Lord has forgiven you, so you also must forgive. And above all these put on love, which binds everything together in perfect harmony. And let the peace of Christ rule in your hearts, to which indeed you were called in one body. And be thankful. (Colossians 3:12–15 ESV)

Notice first in this passage Paul repeats some of the very things you have just been learning about: rejoicing, being thankful, checking your attitude, being kind to others, and not worrying. In Colossians 3:15, Paul adds, "Let the peace of Christ rule in your hearts." Although God wants his children to live with peace of mind, it's up to us to allow his peace to dwell in us. How can his peace dwell in you if you allow your mind to be consumed with all things negative and ungodly?

What do you spend your time thinking about? If you are like me, you think about the same things that you have put into your mind. For instance, when you spend a lot of time around people who curse like sailors, you will find your thoughts are filled with curse words too. What movies do you watch? Are they filled with foul language, illicit sex, and plots of revenge? Then don't be surprised if your mind is occupied much of the time with the same lines of thinking.

There is an old expression, "You are what you eat," which links our state of physical health with what we put into our bodies as fuel. Following that line of thinking, maybe it's time to change the diet of your mind. You will if you are serious about seeking after God's peace of mind. Turn on the gospel music station, and fill your mind with the praises of God more often than the twisted thinking of secular music. Be careful of what you watch on television and at the movies. It's not harmless entertainment. It's feeding your mind an unhealthy diet of lust, greed, and vengeful thoughts. Make a daily habit of reading and studying the Bible. Is there anything better with which to fuel your mind? That daily quiet time with God in prayer and study is perfect for resetting the attitude and preparing you for the day (or repairing you from the day).

Jesus made the comparison using the human eye in Matthew 6:22–23. What you allow to pass by your eyes filters into your soul. If your eyes are busy observing ungodly, unrighteous things, your soul will be full of darkness. But if you fill your eyes with things that bring God glory, then your soul will be full of his light and life.

> The eye is the lamp of the body. So, if your eye is healthy, your whole body will be full of light, but if your eye is bad, your whole body will be full of darkness. If then the light in you is darkness, how great is the darkness! (Matthew 6:22–23 ESV)

> Finally, brothers, whatever is true, whatever is honorable, whatever is just, whatever is pure, whatever is lovely, whatever is commendable, if there is any excellence, if there is anything worthy of praise, think about these things. (Philippians 4:8 ESV)

> We destroy arguments and every lofty opinion raised against the knowledge of God, and take every thought captive to obey Christ. (2 Corinthians 10:5 ESV)

> Put away the evil of your doings from before My eyes, cease to do evil, learn to do good. (Isaiah 1:16–17 NKJV)

> You will keep him in perfect peace whose mind is stayed on You, because he trusts in You. (Isaiah 26:3 NKJV)

You can reclaim your joy and peace of mind, even in the midst of turmoil. I know this to be true! Follow the advice of the apostle Paul. Rejoice in the Lord, for he is worthy to be praised. Strengthen your inner man—give yourself an attitude adjustment so you line up with the Word of God. Get busy showing kindness to others rather than wallowing in your own self-pity. Don't fret or worry about your circumstances or what might happen tomorrow. Trust that God will handle it for you and guide you through it. Begin a new diet for your mind. Fill it with spiritual food and goodness.

> May the God of hope fill you with all joy and peace in believing, so that by the power of the Holy Spirit you may abound in hope. (Romans 15:13 ESV)

# CHAPTER 9

# LEARNING TO FORGIVE

Then Peter came to him and asked, "Lord, how often should I forgive someone who sins against me? Seven times?" (Matthew 18:21 NLT)

If you forgive those who sin against you, your heavenly Father will forgive you. But if you refuse to forgive others, your Father will not forgive your sins. (Matthew 6:14–15 NLT)

Learning to forgive is another aspect of obtaining the peace and joy found in Christ. Forgiveness is a skill that everyone can learn; for Christians, forgiving others is a must. Let's get totally honest. The problem is that, so often, we don't *want* to forgive, yet in Matthew 18:21–35, Jesus taught us to readily forgive, giving us a parable about an unforgiving servant. Jesus would not have commanded something from us that we are unable to do. When Christ lives in us, we can forgive. What we need the most help with is *wanting* and *choosing* to forgive.

Gomer has undeniably hurt you in numerous ways—too many to count. Your trust of Gomer is thin at best. I remember my husband was able to lie while looking me square in the eyes. He regularly made promises that were never kept. I felt tricked, fooled, deceived, and unloved. The decisions he made while addicted brought us to financial ruin and bankruptcy. The lifestyle that swirled around us affected friendships, vacations, and our ability to live a normal life. How many movies, dinners, fun events, holidays, etc. were spoiled or missed altogether due to his mess? Your story is likely similar to mine.

You find yourself becoming angry when you think about those lost or wasted years. It's easy for us Hoseas to hold on to the hurt and anger. The problem is, holding on only serves to keep us from finding the fullness of joy and peace that we are looking for in Christ. Forgiving Gomer is essential, and, with Gomer's history, we have much to forgive. So now you may be asking, "How do I forgive Gomer? Where do I start?"

I find there are many myths about forgiveness that keep people from it. So first, let's shed those myths.

Forgiveness is *not* …

1. Forgiveness doesn't mean forgetting.

Your brain doesn't often forget things, especially those things that hurt you. You may always remember the bad things that happened to you. They are permanently housed in the hard wiring of your brain. Forgiving doesn't magically erase them out of that memory lock. We have somehow combined forgetting with forgiveness, as though we can only forgive when we can forget. So when forgetting doesn't happen, we think we cannot or should not forgive. Here's the truth: even though I have forgiven, if you ask me to tell you about my past hurts, I could recall them with great detail. The difference is whether or not I choose to dwell on them or allow them to dictate my current and/or future actions. Because I have forgiven them, I refuse to allow those past hurts to alter my present or my future. When I recall them, I no longer feel that painful pinch on the inside. I am simply recalling facts, because you asked me.

2. Forgiveness doesn't mean you're a pushover.

Actually, it takes a strong, emotionally healthy person to forgive. Think about this: isn't it a whole lot easier to hold a grudge than to forgive? So then, each time you forgive, you are showing a great deal of personal strength, demonstrating your spiritual muscles. When you forgive, you are a better person. You gain the upper hand by not allowing the hurt to continue hurting. It's like taking all the ammunition away from a sniper.

The sniper still exists and is waving his old weapon around in a threatening manner. You even remember the sniper, but now the sniper cannot hurt you anymore. He has no bullets! You look at the sniper with a knowing smile.

3. Forgiving doesn't mean you no longer feel angry or hurt.

Even Christ felt anger. The difference is, when he was angry he was able to keep his actions pleasing before God. He didn't allow feelings of anger to determine his actions. Yes, you hurt me. Yes, I may still be angry remembering what you did, but I refuse to let this stand between my God and me. I will demonstrate forgiveness by acting righteously toward you, because Christ has freely forgiven me. It may take some time for the hurt and the anger to dissolve as the spirit heals me on the inside, but, in the meantime, my actions toward you will be right before God.

4. Forgiving doesn't mean you will reconcile.

Forgiving others doesn't change who they are; forgiveness changes *you*. Just because you have decided to forgive Gomer doesn't mean Gomer will necessarily be a part of your life like he was before. Sometimes, even though you forgave someone, you may realize that person is not someone with whom you want to continue a close relationship. For instance, forgiving someone of all the past lies doesn't automatically make that person honest and truthful. Forgiveness clears the old slate, true, so you don't keep bringing it all up, but you may decide not to trust what that person says in the future (wisdom). Therefore, a full relationship with that person may not be reconcilable until true and long-term changes occur. Another example is when hurt feelings run both ways: you may have forgiven someone, but he is unwilling to forgive you. This relationship is split, even though you did your part in forgiving him. That's all you can do. Pray for these people.

5. Forgiving doesn't mean the person deserves it.

We often feel like we can forgive only when the person has suffered enough and has begged for it while crawling over broken glass. But forgiveness has nothing to do with him. The bottom line is this: no matter what that person does now, no matter what we put that person through because we are hurt and angry, none of this changes or erases the sin against us. Only forgiveness has the power to cover it. We don't deserve to be forgiven by Christ. He forgives us in his great mercy only—not because we have earned it, not because we are worthy of his forgiveness. As a Christian who is learning to model your life after Christ, you too must choose to forgive others purely because of mercy, never because they deserve it.

> Don't copy the behavior and customs of this world, but let God transform you into a new person by changing the way you think. Then you will learn to know God's will for you, which is good and pleasing and perfect. (Romans 12:2 NLT)

Now, let's transform our minds; letting go of the myths, let us discover the truth about forgiveness.

Forgiveness *is* ...

1. Forgiveness is perhaps the most like Christ you can be.

"But God shows his love for us in that while we were still sinners, Christ died for us" (Romans 5:8 ESV). Do you really want to be like Christ? Then forgive those who sin against you, who purposefully treat you badly, who rejoice in your suffering. Not only forgive them, but also love them and treat them kindly. This is right behavior. Be like Christ; forgive Gomer.

2. Forgiving is a choice

Don't go on feelings. You will never *feel* like forgiving, so you can't wait for that. It is a choice you make based on Christ-like mercy. Choose to forgive Gomer.

3. Forgiving is a learned behavior.

It doesn't come naturally to our flesh. It is something you must practice. It will come easier over time, as all learned behaviors do and as your spirit man grows in strength. Show you are growing in Christ; forgive Gomer.

4. Forgiveness is an effort.

It isn't easy. You will struggle with it, but it must be done. Don't give up on it, thinking you can't do it. In life, anything really worth doing takes effort. Forgiveness is worth the effort. It is worth it to you; forgive Gomer.

5. Forgiveness is merciful.

Gomer doesn't deserve to be forgiven. Exactly! This is mercy in its purest form. If he deserved it, then forgiveness wouldn't really be necessary, nor would it be merciful. Although trust must be earned, forgiveness is simply undeserved. Be merciful; forgive Gomer.

6. Forgiveness is healthy for you.

Holding grudges (refusing to forgive) has been proven to increase blood pressure, reduce sleep quality, cause ulcers, and many other physical ailments. Forgiving others releases your body from all these internal stresses. Be healthy; forgive Gomer.

7. Forgiveness is freedom.

Why carry around the weight of anger, hurt, pain, etc.? When you forgive Gomer, this weight drops off over time, giving you emotional freedom. The most relaxed, carefree, and rested feeling you will ever experience comes as you forgive from the heart. Be free! Forgive Gomer!

8. Forgiveness is power and control.

When you don't forgive, the hurtful, painful actions of Gomer control your emotional state of mind. Gomer pulls your strings; he pushes your buttons. He pulls them anytime and as often as he wants. But when you forgive Gomer, you are in control of your emotions again. No matter what Gomer does against you, he no longer has that destructive power over you. Forgiving Gomer gives you complete control over your feelings and power over your own emotions. Take back control; forgive Gomer.

9. Forgiveness is necessary.

Jesus said it quite bluntly in Matthew 6:14–15. He also told a parable about forgiveness in Matthew 18:21–35. Jesus went even further in Luke 6:27–36, teaching we are not only to forgive but also to treat even our enemies with love. We are to bless them and pray for those who do us wrong. Now don't let this scare you—forgive Gomer first in shear obedience to Christ. Your heart may not seem to be in it to begin with, but show God you are committed to obeying him in all things. Christ, who lives in you, will warm your heart, strengthening you to do the rest as time goes by. Be obedient; forgive Gomer.

10. Forgiveness is endless.

People are sinful by nature. First of all, most people, including those who go to church—even those who call themselves Christians—are often not living lives overly pleasing to God. Therefore, they are doing things that have the potential to be hurtful to you. This isn't going to end as long as we are living on this earth. You've lived it with Gomer; it's an endless cycle of sin, hurt, and forgiveness. Sometimes the same person needs your forgiveness over and over. Other times, a variety of people at varying times will need your forgiveness. Some people honestly desire to be forgiven; they are truly sorry they have hurt you. Other people are calloused and take pleasure in seeing you hurt. But for all the reasons already mentioned in numbers above, you need to forgive others even if they don't seek your forgiveness. So you might as well learn to forgive; you'll be practicing it your entire life. Start practicing; forgive Gomer.

11. Forgiving is really self-motivated.

Let's think about ourselves for a minute. Forgiving other people is one of the best things you can do for *you*. If it helps, stop thinking of it as a gift to others. In truth, you're giving yourself a gift in spite of them! If they meant to hurt you and you forgive them, this ruins their day, because you were supposed to be all upset and lose sleep. But instead of your day being ruined, you remain happy and at peace. Do you see how forgiveness is really more about you than about them? Jesus wants you to forgive, because he knows what's best for you! Do what is best for *you*; forgive Gomer.

12. Forgiving is a process.

Only God is able to truly forgive instantaneously. The more mature and Christlike we become, the quicker the process of forgiving others will become in us. For new Christians, and especially when desiring to forgive the deepest, most painful hurts, it seems more like a wrestling match between our flesh and our spirit, a process of renewal that occurs over time. First comes the realization that forgiveness is necessary. We wrestle with that until we decide, in the mercy and example of Christ, to forgive. Then we struggle to go through with it. Much prayer and daily effort are needed to release the hurt, anger, and destructive thoughts our human nature wants to hold on to. Over time, the Holy Spirit in us will purge these out of us if we are willing to let them go. The deeper the hurt, the longer this process tends to be. Start the process; forgive Gomer.

> Brethren, I do not count myself to have apprehended; but one thing *I do*, forgetting those things which are behind and reaching forward to those things which are ahead, I press toward the goal for the prize of the upward call of God in Christ Jesus. Therefore let us, as many as are mature, have this mind; and if in anything you think otherwise, God will reveal even this to you. Nevertheless, to *the degree* that we have already attained, let us walk by the same rule, let us be of the same mind. (Philippians 3:13–16 NKJV)

# CHAPTER 10

# HOLDING ON TO HOPE

Why are you cast down, O my soul?
And why are you disquieted within me?
Hope in God;
For I shall yet praise Him,
The help of my countenance and my God.
(Psalm 42:11 NKJV)

There may be times that it seems all hope is gone. Gomer is never going to quit using. Life is never going to be any better. Satan would have you believe you may as well just kill yourself, that even if you leave Gomer, your own life won't improve anyway. Nobody understands or really cares about you. I remember thinking all these things numerous times. Do not fall into Satan's trap of hopelessness. You will only find endless despair waiting for you there.

Let me encourage you. Part of what Jesus tells us in Matthew 19:23–26 (NKJV) is, "But with God all things are possible." This doesn't mean it will be easy. This doesn't mean it will happen the very day or week you ask God for help. This doesn't mean you and Gomer won't separate. It *does* mean that God is able to carry you through whatever your future brings, if you lean on him. When someone is drowning and you try to rescue him, if he doesn't relax and let you do the swimming, he is still likely to drown during the rescue attempt. Relax and let God do the swimming. Go in whatever direction he leads you. His guidance will always lead to a peaceful shore.

> We were given this hope when we were saved. (If we already have something, we don't need to hope for it. But if we look forward to something we don't yet have, we must wait patiently and confidently.) (Romans 8:24–25 NLT)

What is hope? Is hope any different from faith? They have the same basic meaning but with two different degrees of expectation. Hope is at least a slight expectation of obtaining something in the future. It is the belief that something is possibly obtainable. Faith is complete unwavering trust or confidence. Faith ups the degree of expectation. In the world, we can only have hope; but in God, we can put our faith. The Bible is full of Scriptures which exhort, give hope, and build our faith in Christ. Read Hebrews chapter 11. Read all of it. This chapter is often referred to as the "Faith Hall of Fame."

Often, the word "patience" is found in Scriptures that talk about faith. In other words, we must have enduring and unshakable faith, knowing what we expect to obtain won't happen overnight. Just because it could take years, we do not lose sight. God is faithful. His promises are true. Therefore, I continue to expect to receive what God has actually promised.

Do you know what has God promised? Here is where many people remain disconnected from the source. How can you know what to expect from God if you don't know what he has promised? Let's fix that problem. The following pages will give you a good starting point. The Bible is so full of promises that I cannot tell you all of them, but I will give you some highlights. You may choose to write down personal notes in the margins and write down additional Scriptures as you find them.

*Jesus promised he would return.*
I know it seems as if he is never going to return, but you must understand he desires everyone to accept his gift of salvation. So he is ever patient, giving mankind more time to choose him.

2 Peter 3:8–13
John 14:1–3, 18, 28

1 Thessalonians 4:13–18
Isaiah 65:17

*Jesus promised to never leave nor forsake us.*
When it seems that he is nowhere around, make sure you didn't walk away
from him. He is faithful to us. We are often not so faithful to him. Walk
quickly back in his direction and take hold of his hand once again.

Matthew 28:20
Psalm 139:1–14
Proverbs 10:25
Joshua 1:9
Deuteronomy 31:8
John 14:16–17

*Jesus promised to give us the strength needed for righteous living.*
You may not want to deal with the problems that come your way, but he
promised he would not allow you to go through anything that would be
too much for you to handle *with* his strength and guidance.

Psalm 27:13–14
1 Corinthians 10:12–13
Jeremiah 17:7–8
Lamentations 3:22–57
Isaiah 40:28–31
Isaiah 55:6–9
Psalm 37:39–40
Isaiah 41:17–20
Psalm 55:22
Psalm 18:1–3
Hebrews 4:14–16

*Jesus promised to be our refuge and place of comfort.*
Many people get mad at God when life isn't what they had hoped for
or expected it to be. This seems especially true when tragedy strikes
them personally or strikes someone in their family. But life is hard for

everyone—only those serving the Lord have the privilege and comfort of knowing he is there to help.

Psalm 91:1–16
Psalm 46:1–5
Psalm 9:9–10
John 16:33
Matthew 11:28

*Jesus promised you wouldn't have to fight your battles alone.*
You, child of God, are never alone. God and his army of angels are ready to fight for righteousness to prevail. Allow this promise to fill you with confidence in the face of trouble.

2 Kings 6:16–17
Philippians 4:13
Luke 18:7–8
Psalm 27:1–5
Psalm 60:11–12
Isaiah 43:1–2

*Jesus promised to meet the needs of the faithful.*
God is able to provide for you, even when you can't see how. When you feel your faith starting to waver, start reciting God's promises back to him. He must and will keep his promises. Just make sure you are keeping your end of faithfulness to him.

Psalm 37:23–25
Matthew 6:25–34
Matthew 7:11
2 Corinthians 4:16–18
Joel 2:25–27

*Jesus promised you will find peace, rest, and joy in him.*
All his promises are true, even this one. Follow the principles he set forth in the Bible. Review chapter 8 in this book if you need help finding peace

and joy. You will soon be amazed at the level of peace, rest, and joy you have in him.

Matthew 11:28–30
Psalm 1:1–6
Romans 15:13
John 14:27
John 15:9–11
Philippians 4:6–7
Colossians 3:15
Psalm 85:8–13
Psalm 126:5–6
Nehemiah 8:10
Isaiah 32:17–18
Isaiah 55:8–12
Isaiah 61:1–3

*Jesus promised your work in his kingdom will be successful if you don't give up.* Please realize that success in his kingdom is not promised unless you follow the principles of God. Do not give up on the promises. Be forever careful not to get so full of yourself that you claim this promise of God while ignoring the rest of the Bible. It is, after all, a package deal.

Galatians 6:9
2 Chronicles 15:7
1 Peter 5:6–11
1 Corinthians 15:58

CHAPTER 11

# FINDING COMFORT

Would you like a hug? A big shoulder to cry on? I can imagine the pain you feel in your innermost being while you watch Gomer drown in his addiction. If I could talk to each of you personally, I would try to comfort you with that hug you desire. In John 14:15–18, Christ offers comfort to those of us who accept him as Lord. He sent the Holy Spirit as our earthly comforter. Jesus Christ himself knew before he was crucified that he would not always be able to be physically present with his followers. He knew we would need his comfort as his people have from days of old.

> So the ransomed of the Lord shall return, and come to Zion with singing, with everlasting joy on their heads. They shall obtain joy and gladness; sorrow and sighing shall flee away. "I, even I, am He who comforts you." (Isaiah 51:11–12 NKJVJ)

Is it comforting to know that you are not alone, that you are not the only person who has a Gomer in her life? In a strange way, I found it comforting to know others are out there with similar stories; although it never made my personal anguish any less painful. I talked to others and went to group meetings for a time. These things comforted me while I was there with them, but once I was home, alone, their comfort was gone.

God, through His Holy Spirit is able to comfort you when nobody else can. Think about Jesus' life on this earth. He was rejected and crucified by the very people whom he had healed out of compassion. He was mocked and spat upon by the same people he had fed on the hillside. Was there even one person who stood by him in his worst moment? Jesus felt what it was like to be hated, mocked, ridiculed, used, rejected, isolated, and tired. That's why he sent the comforter. He knows how badly we need him. He knows how badly *you* need him.

Paul writes to Timothy about a time when not a single friend stood by him when he needed them the most in 2 Timothy 4:9–18. Paul and Luke asked for help to come in a hurry (verse 9). But Paul recognized in verse 17 that the Lord had never forsaken him; rather, the Lord had strengthened him so he could bear it. Paul further describes his many troubles and imprisonments as a Christian in 2 Corinthians 11:23–33. In 2 Corinthians 12:10, Paul states that he prefers to take pleasure (even comfort) in his troubles, because during these times of weakness he utilizes Christ's strength rather than his own.

Mankind as a whole is arrogant in thinking that they don't need God. We can, after all, "heal" people through miracle drugs and surgeries that we ourselves think we created. We can build rockets to explore space and microscopes to examine the atom. We believe we have the power and the right to create (i.e. test tube babies) and to destroy (i.e. abortion). We believe we can know the future (i.e. psychics). Mankind likes to believe that we don't need God for anything really. More and more humans believe that we ourselves are gods who can control our own destinies, that if we stand before God one day, we won't be answering his questions—he will be the one answering questions. You may think this, that is, until you find yourself in a situation that is truly out of your control. What are the first words that come to mind? "Oh God! Help me!" Whether you are a self-proclaimed atheist or not, when you honestly believe you are faced with imminent death, you cry out to God, the maker of your soul.

It's hard to take joy from our trials even though we know that in the end we will be better, stronger people for having gone through them. We'd rather just not go through them. And yet, God allows trials to come into our lives so we may prove God's greatness once again. Think about the story of Job in the Bible. He didn't deserve (from the human perspective) the trials that he suffered, even though his friends assumed it must somehow be his own fault. God allowed Satan to severely attack Job's family, wealth, and health in order that God's goodness would shine through in the end. How would we truly know God's goodness if he never had to help us through anything? Even so, this concept of God allowing us to suffer in order to know his goodness is difficult for us to comprehend or accept.

Christ, the very Son of God, was not above trials and temptations, so what makes us think we shouldn't have any? Christians need to change their line of thinking. Instead of complaining, "God, why have you allowed this to happen to me?" we should be praising him: "Thank you, God, for helping me through this and using it to make me a more faithful follower of Christ." God inhabits the praises of his people. He grew angry when the Israelites complained. When you are going through a rough time and the only help you can find is in God, do you want him angry, because you are complaining? Or do you want to draw him close to you along with the help only he can bring?

> So let us come boldly to the throne of our gracious God.
> There we will receive his mercy, and we will find grace to
> help us when we need it most. (Hebrews 4:16 NLT)

When you are faced with a trial, honestly ask yourself, "Did I bring this on myself?" Oftentimes we suffer due to our own actions, our own choices. Maybe it was a decision you made without God's counsel or approval. Maybe you are simply reaping what you have sown. If so, repent. Ask God to guide you through this. Learn from it, so next time you are faced with a decision, you will remember to pray for God's guidance and wait for him to lead you.

> And remember, when you are being tempted, do not say,
> "God is tempting me." God is never tempted to do wrong,
> and he never tempts anyone else. Temptation comes from
> our own desires, which entice us and drag us away. These
> desires give birth to sinful actions. And when sin is allowed
> to grow, it gives birth to death. (James 1:13–15 NLT)

In Romans 5:1–5 (NLT), Paul tells us, "We can rejoice, too, when we run into problems and trials, for we know that they help us develop endurance." Many Christians, though, instead of getting a surge of hope, feel pity (or even anger) that God has allowed yet another trial. Paul says here that tribulations reveal our Christlike character, or lack of it, more than anything else can. Character and hope are strengthened through tribulations. With each successive trial, we should have greater hope and faith in the God we serve, Jesus Christ our Lord and Savior. We know he brought us safely through the last trial, and the trial before that, and the trial before that; so we know he can, and will, bring us through again.

Jeremiah 18:6 reminds us that God is the potter shaping his children as clay into a more Christlike image. What does a potter do to the clay figure once it is finished? He bakes it in the kiln. Our trials are meant to firm us up in the Lord. It's a great time to prove to God and to others that you have become more like Christ, that you've learned the lessons he wanted you to learn. If you don't hold up under the heat of the trial, and you are broken, then you must be reshaped yet again by the potter. He doesn't give up on us; he lovingly works again at molding us.

Often our trials are intended to reveal to *us* the areas we need to work on. God already knows, but because of our arrogance, they need to be exposed for us to see them. For example, we may think we are patient until a situation arises where we must really use patience. We may discover we are not so patient after all! A patient Savior is needed to live in me, helping me every hour!

Take your comfort in Christ. He isn't up in heaven watching you suffer with a smirk on his face, saying, "I'd like to see him get himself out of this one." That is not the God of my Bible. That is a lie from Satan. The truth is that God, with Jesus on his right hand, is dwelling in you as the Holy Spirit, your comforter and teacher through times of trouble, ever ready, willing, and able to help you. Have you asked him? Continue to pray and seek his face until he answers, and relief comes. He has promised, and he is faithful.

> In You, O Lord, I put my trust;
> Let me never be put to shame.
> Deliver me in your righteousness, and cause me to escape;
> Incline Your ear to me, and save me.
> Be my strong refuge,

To which I may resort continually;
You have given the commandment to save me,
For You are my rock and my fortress.
(Psalm 71:1–3 NKJV)

# CHAPTER 12

# THE COURAGE TO CONTINUE

The Spirit indeed is willing, but the flesh is weak."
(Matthew 26:41 NKJV)

Do you want to keep trying? This is the question that only you can answer. It's hard to keep going when you don't even have the finish line in view. It's even harder to keep struggling when you know there is no finish line—when your heart says that you are not ready to completely give up on Gomer and walk away, yet you don't have the emotional strength to keep going. Where does the courage to continue come from?

> But I will hope continually,
> And will praise You yet more and more.
> My mouth shall tell of Your righteousness
> And Your salvation all the day,
> For I do not know their limits.
> I will go in the strength of the Lord God;
> I will make mention of Your righteousness, of Yours only.
> (Psalm 71:14–16 NKJV)

David penned those words during a time of distress. To me, they mean except for God's strength, I would not have the strength to continue. But I *can* go on, because the Lord gives me strength. David also mentions here how to unlock this strength from on high—it comes from praising God. I wrote to you about worshipping God in chapter 8. Having the courage to continue is strongly related to your levels of joy and peace. When you maintain your joy in the Lord, you find that the courage to keep on keeping on is not difficult to grasp. Courage is illusive when there is no peace or joy.

This is common sense stuff. Who wants to continue in something that is making them miserable? When you reclaim your joy and peace in Jesus—instead of connected to your circumstances—then you can keep up the good fight for Gomer's very soul. King David even wanted to quit. What stopped him? Only his faith in God:

> A Psalm of David.
> The Lord is my light and my salvation;
> Whom shall I fear?
> The Lord is the strength of my life;
> Of whom shall I be afraid?
> I would have lost heart, unless I had believed
> That I would see the goodness of the Lord
> In the land of the living.
> Wait on the Lord;
> Be of good courage,
> And He shall strengthen your heart;
> Wait, I say, on the Lord!
> (Psalm 27:1, 13–14 NKJV)

Let's look at another example from the Bible:

Joshua was appointed by God to replace Moses as leader of Israel after Moses' death. The task of leading such a large band of unruly, stiff-necked people must have been daunting. Moses had been their only leader, and he had led them for forty years. Would the people listen to Joshua, such a relatively young man, such a new leader? I'm sure Joshua must have wondered, too, if God would work miracles through him as he did with Moses.

Perhaps Joshua felt there was someone else more worthy of the position than he was. The Bible doesn't specifically record Joshua seeking after Moses' position. It doesn't record Joshua asking to be the next leader. But it does tell us in Exodus 33:11 (NKJV) that Joshua "did not depart from the tabernacle" seeking after God's presence.

> And the Lord, He is the One who goes before you. He will be with you, He will not leave you nor forsake you; do not fear nor be dismayed. (Deuteronomy 31:8 NKJV)

> Have I not commanded you? Be strong and of good courage; do not be afraid, nor be dismayed, for the Lord your God is with you wherever you go. (Joshua 1:9 NKJV)

God commanded Joshua, immediately following the death of Moses, not to be afraid or dismayed. Why? How could God expect Joshua to not be overwhelmed? Because the task was not Joshua's to handle. God was the real leader. All Joshua had to do was whatever the Lord asked of him—step by step, faith to faith.

I'm sure you never hoped or wanted to deal with a Gomer. I'm sure you never prayed, "Lord, I sure wish I could have the problem of a Gomer to deal with in this life." Like Joshua, perhaps, you didn't seek this "position." Regardless, God has seen fit to allow this burden to be placed on you, or maybe your own poor choices have led you into this wilderness. Nevertheless, he wants to handle it for you. Gomer is not *your* problem to "fix." Gomer is God's problem, and God doesn't need your help. All the courage you need is to keep on trusting God and allow him to lead you in all that you do.

Pray continually. Do whatever the Lord lays on your heart to do concerning Gomer. The principles in this book are only guidelines. Please know that God will never lead you to act contrary to his word or character. Become familiar with the words and meanings of the Bible. Get to know the God you serve personally; it makes following him easier!

Paul continued this line of thinking:

> But we have this treasure in earthen vessels that the excellence of the power may be of God and not of us. (2 Corinthians 4:7 NKJV)

The "earthen vessels" Paul is speaking of are referring to you and me—human beings—saved by grace. We are God's chosen vessels. What then is the treasure that is in us? The Holy Spirit is our treasure, which was promised to come to us to comfort and teach us all things needed for the furtherance of the gospel message (John 14:7–13, 16). What is the power Paul is speaking of? It is the power to heal the brokenhearted, to set the captives free, to preach the gospel, to comfort those who mourn and turn their sorrow into joy, to take away heaviness and replace it with praise all for the glory of God (Isaiah 61:1–3). Paul says there is excellence in this power, but it is only because of God's greatness. It has nothing to do with our abilities. Read what Paul says next:

> We are hard pressed on every side, yet not crushed; we are perplexed, but not in despair; persecuted, but not forsaken; struck down, but not destroyed. (2 Corinthians 4:8–9 NKJV)

Is Paul saying that while we have this power in us we will still go through trying times? Yes! But the burdens do not crush us anymore when we allow the power of God to handle them. We don't have to feel despair, because we know that God will see us through. We know we are not forsaken because the spirit in us testifies to us that God is with us, just as he promised he would be. We are never destroyed, because we know we are more than conquerors through Christ Jesus (Romans 8:31). Suddenly the trials of life take on a whole new light.

When we first start working out, our muscles ache, and we usually dread getting back on the exercise machines. Why do we do it? To get physically fit. No pain, no gain, right? Trials are like a spiritual workout facility provided through God's ultimate wisdom. It's really a controlled environment with a personal trainer and physician—a spiritual stress test, if you will. Trials are spiritual workouts. They test our endurance in Christ. The test is really about *you* realizing where you are in your walk with God. How much do you trust him? The Lord knows already exactly where we are. He knows we are weak (Luke 8:22–25), but often we need to know ourselves and be shown our real areas of weakness. The trials leave us stronger, if we don't quit. We don't have to dread our trials anymore, because we understand their overall purpose. We get the big picture, and so we look forward to growing stronger in the Lord.

> If you faint in the day of adversity, your strength is small.
> (Proverbs 24:10 NKJV)

That Scripture is not meant as a criticism—it's given as a fact. In the natural world, if you can't lift ten pounds then your strength would be described as small. In the spiritual world, if you cannot stand on God's word in faith, then your spiritual strength is small. Perhaps you are a babe in Christ. Then spiritually speaking, you have growing and strengthening to do. Don't be ashamed that your strength is small. You're a new believer in Christ, and less strength is expected from children. Give yourself time to grow. As you grow by studying God's word, you will get stronger!

If you've been saved for a while and you are still spiritually weak, then it's time you get honest with yourself. Dig into God's word like never before, and get the spiritual nourishment that develops into spiritual muscles as you exercise, putting God's word into action in your life. If you know God's word but don't exercise it, then you will stay weak. I own and know how to use my exercise equipment at home, but unless I actually *use* it regularly, it does me no good. I will remain physically weak and out of shape.

Life has natural ups and downs. There will be very difficult and trying times that seem never-ending. But they will end. During this time, it is said you are hiking up the mountain. If you stop climbing altogether, your only alternatives are to return to the valley (that's not a good place) or to stay put (stagnate). Neither of these is a good choice. When you tire from the climb, it's perfectly okay to rest a while. You don't have to give up climbing completely! Nor must you feel discouraged and disheartened that you need to rest. You are merely resting. Just be careful while you rest that you don't turn aside from following after God's will for you. Rest a while, and then get back up and start climbing again.

> Suddenly a voice came to him and said, "What are you doing here, Elijah?" And he said, "I have been very zealous for the Lord God of Hosts; because the children of Israel

have forsaken Your covenant, torn down Your altars, and killed Your prophets with the sword, I alone am left; and they seek to take my life." Then the Lord said to him: "Go, return on your way ..." (1 Kings 19:13–15 NKJV)

And do not run aside; for then you would go after empty things which cannot profit or deliver, for they are nothing. For the Lord will not forsake His people; for His great name's sake, because it has pleased the Lord to make you His people. (1 Samuel 12:21–22 NKJV)

It seems to be part of our human nature to forget God when times are good. We quickly turn arrogant, convincing ourselves and others that the prosperity we are enjoying is due solely to our personal greatness. We are so talented, gifted, wise, and intelligent. We planned and worked to get to this place. We too easily forget that except for the grace of God, our circumstances could be very different.

You have been a strength to the poor,
A strength to the needy in his distress,
A refuge from the storm,
A shade from the heat.
(Isaiah 25:4 NKJV)

Perhaps it's due to our very tendency to live our daily lives without asking God to play an active role in them that God allows as many trials to come our way as he does. After all, he wants us to rely on him. He wants us to commune daily—continually even—with him. If allowing us to go through a trial quickly turns our focus back to him—so we talk and worship with him more, and remember to say "I love you, Lord"—then so be it.

# CHAPTER 13

# SPIRITUAL WARFARE (DON'T BECOME SATAN'S POW)

> For we are not fighting against flesh-and-blood enemies,
> but against evil rulers and authorities of the unseen world,
> against mighty powers in this dark world, and against evil
> spirits in the heavenly places. (Ephesians 6:12 NLT)

Addiction is a spiritual battle—a stronghold. As a Hosea, you are a soldier (probably drafted against your will) who must wage spiritual warfare against the addiction and the slew of problems that come with it. Participating in physical battles with the addict, such as fighting, yelling, and cursing, will not win this war. It won't even win a single battle. It's often difficult to remember this when the addict screams in your face, but it is true. You must learn to separate your love for the addict from your hate of the addiction. The more you understand addiction (refer back to Section One of this book) the easier it will be to have true compassion for the addict's seeming inability to stop and the less his irrational behavior will send you into a tailspin.

> No one engaged in warfare entangles himself with the
> affairs of this life, that he may please him who enlisted
> him as a soldier. (2 Timothy 2:4 NKJV)

> For though we walk in the flesh, we do not war according to the flesh. For the weapons of our warfare are not carnal but mighty in God for pulling down strongholds, casting down arguments and every high thing that exalts itself against the knowledge of God, bringing every thought into captivity to the obedience of Christ. (2 Corinthians 10:3–5 NKJV)

Since we are wrestling against spiritual powers, how do we begin to battle addiction? First, read Ephesians 6:10–18. As we look at it more closely, you will notice it can be summed up into three sentences: Be strong. Put on the whole armor of God. Know the enemy. Now, let's delve into each part more closely.

## 1. Be Strong (Ephesians 6:10)

Any battle, if you wish to survive, requires strength in body and in mind. Soldiers for the US Army go to boot camp and undergo rigorous training to promote physical strength and mental fortitude. Without them both, they would easily die, run away from the battle, or be more easily killed by the enemy. But where do we get strength for such a spiritual battle?

Read 1 Samuel 17:32–50.

The story of David and Goliath is powerful and much more than a story for children! Although it is a physical battle, David did not win by his own physical prowess. In fact, Goliath laughed at David and considered him a stick, a little boy (verse 43). David merely replied that he wouldn't be fighting Goliath with his own strength but instead with the power of God who does not fight using swords and spears (verse 47)!

Confidence in the Lord like that of David is real strength! The Bible tells us how to achieve this level of confidence. Here are just a few passages to get you going:

## Let God handle it:

❖ God will do a better job anyway. Let him deal with it (you must pray).

❖ Aren't you tired of trying to handle the mess by now anyway?

Each time he said, "My grace is all you need. My power works best in weakness." So now I am glad to boast about my weaknesses, so that the power of Christ can work through me. (2 Corinthians 12:9 NLT)

**Pray:**

❖ God does hear and answer our prayers.
❖ Each prayer answered serves to strengthen our confidence in God's willingness to intercede and help us.

In the day when I cried out, You answered me, and made me bold with strength in my soul. (Psalm 138:3 NKJV)

**Trust God:**

❖ This is faith in its raw form. Believe God will help you.
❖ Trusting and praying go hand-in-hand.

Don't be afraid, for I am with you. Don't be discouraged, for I am your God. I will strengthen you and help you. I will hold you up with my victorious right hand. (Isaiah 41:10 NLT)

**Use God's wisdom:**

❖ What seems wise to us may not be very wise in God's eyes after all.
❖ Seek God's counsel as Solomon did before he was anointed the King of Israel. (See 1 Kings 3:5–28 and 4:29–34 NLT)

Wisdom strengthens the wise more than ten rulers of the city. (Ecclesiastes 7:19 NKJV)

**Have patience:**

❖ Understand your prayers will be answered in God's time.
❖ Answers may not come overnight.
❖ Learn to wait without doubting.

> He gives power to the weak, and to those who have no might He increases strength. Even the youths shall faint and be weary, and the young men shall utterly fall, but those who wait upon the Lord shall renew their strength; they shall mount up with wings like eagles, they shall run and not be weary, they shall walk and not faint. (Isaiah 40:31 NKJV)

**Know your advocate (Jesus):**

❖ Learn more through regular Bible study.
❖ The better you know him, the easier it will be to trust him and wait patiently.

> But the Lord stood with me and strengthened me, so that the message might be preached fully through me, and that all the Gentiles might hear. Also I was delivered out of the mouth of the lion. And the Lord will deliver me from every evil work and preserve me for His heavenly kingdom. To Him be glory forever and ever. Amen! (2 Timothy 4:17–18 NKJV)

**Press on with God through the hard times:**

❖ When you mess up and fail God, get back up instead of giving up.
❖ Learn to run to God in the hard times rather than getting mad at him.

> And the Lord said, "Simon, Simon! Indeed, Satan has asked for you, that he may sift you as wheat. But I have prayed for you, that your faith should not fail; and when

you have returned to Me, strengthen your brethren."
(Luke 22:31–32 NKJV)

**Grow mature in God's word:**

- ❖ Start by learning the foundations of the Christian faith.
- ❖ Maturing is a daily, lifelong process. Expect a few growing pains.
- ❖ As a believer, you should know what the Bible says about salvation, baptism, the Holy Spirit, communion, church attendance, tithing, the armor of God, and the fruits of the Spirit. That's what it means to be rooted and grounded. Then move into deeper studies of God's Word.

For this reason I bow my knees to the Father of our Lord Jesus Christ, from whom the whole family in heaven and earth is named, that He would grant you, according to the riches of His glory, to be strengthened with might through His Spirit in the inner man that Christ may dwell in your hearts through faith; that you, being rooted and grounded in love, may be able to comprehend with all the saints what is the width and length and height; to know the love of Christ which surpasses knowledge; that you may be filled with all the fullness of God. (Ephesians 3:14–19 NKJV)

## 2. Put on the Whole Armor of God (Ephesians 6:11, 13–17)

Every soldier protects himself with armor, because he expects the battle to be dangerous. During war, military personnel are known to protect themselves with gas masks, bulletproof clothing, tanks, trenches, and the like. Physical battles are not easy or peaceful. We should not expect a spiritual battle to be a piece of cake either. What is spiritual armor? I'm so glad you asked:

**The Truth Girdle**

Stand therefore, having girded your waist with truth …
(Ephesians 6:14 NKJV)

I like this reference to a girdle. When you first start restricting your lifestyle, habits, and desires to match the truth—that is, the Word of God—you feel like you are wearing a girdle. Each time you do something that doesn't line up with God's Word as you understand it, you will feel the girdle cut into you. The truth girdle, in essence, contains the very boundaries of your Christian walk. God's Word tells us what is and is not permissible. And moreover, these boundaries are focused largely on internal measures of attitude, intent, and heart. Ouch! The more you line up with the Word of God, the less often you will notice the girdle pressing into your life. With time, the truth girdle will seem less burdensome as your habits and desires change. Living according to the Word of God is a spiritual defense, a piece of your armor. Start wearing it.

> Then Jesus said to those Jews who believed Him, "If you abide in My word, you are My disciples indeed. And you shall know the truth and the truth shall make you free." (John 8:31–32 NKJV)

> Sanctify them by Your truth. Your word is truth. As You sent Me into the world, I also have sent them into the world. And for their sakes I sanctify Myself, that they also may be sanctified by the truth. (John 17:17–19 NKJV)

> That we should no longer be children, tossed to and fro and carried about with every wind of doctrine, by the trickery of men, in the cunning craftiness of deceitful plotting, but speaking the truth in love, may grow up in all things into Him who is the head—Christ. (Ephesians 4:14–15 NKJV)

### The Blame-Proof Vest of Righteousness

> Having put on the breastplate of righteousness ... (Ephesians 6:14 NKJV)

How do you become blameless? Must you be perfect? No, certainly not, or none of us would attain it. The grace of God covers our sins. When we do sin, the truth girdle lets us know. It's important to recognize our sins and repent. Repentance implies turning away from the sin. You can't just say you are sorry and ask God to forgive you with your lips only, while in your heart you know you will do the same sin again when the opportunity presents itself. God looks on the heart. True repentance—and therefore, blamelessness—reflects the true condition of your heart. It reflects your willingness and intention to try.

Being blameless also requires you to do the things that you know you should do. It's more than just not doing sinful acts; it's performing good acts, too. We are told throughout Scripture to feed the hungry, give to the needy, be kind, be compassionate, loving, etc. We will not be held blameless if we are unwilling to portray these qualities of Christ through our actions, with our hearts, our time, and our resources.

The same goes for putting the talents that God has given us to use furthering the gospel. We will be held accountable if we waste those talents or refuse to put them to use in God's kingdom. We are not designed to sit on the sidelines, only warming a pew every Sunday. He has placed talents, abilities, and opportunities in your life. Discover them, acknowledge them, and start using them!

> Remember, it is sin to know what you ought to do and then not do it. (James 4:17 NLT)

> Then He will also say to those on the left hand, "Depart from Me, you cursed, into everlasting fire prepared for the devil and his angels: for I was hungry and you gave Me no food; I was thirsty and you gave Me no drink; I was a stranger and you did not take Me in, naked and you did not clothe Me, sick and in prison and you did not visit Me." (Matthew 25:41–43 NKJV)

> "And I was afraid, and went and hid Your talent in the ground. Look, there you have what is yours." But his lord answered and said to him, "You wicked and lazy servant ... therefore take the talent from him, and give it to him who has ten talents ... and cast the unprofitable

servant into outer darkness." There will be weeping and gnashing of teeth. (Matthew 25:25–26, 28, 30 NKJV)

Dear friends, I warn you as "temporary residents and foreigners" to keep away from worldly desires that wage war against your very souls. Be careful to live properly among your unbelieving neighbors. Then even if they accuse you of doing wrong, they will see your honorable behavior, and they will give honor to God when he judges the world. (1 Peter 2:11–12 NLT)

Be sober, reverent, temperate, sound in faith, in love, in patience; … reverent in behavior, not slanderers, not given to much wine, teachers of good things, … sober-minded, in all things showing yourself to be a pattern of good works; in doctrine showing integrity, reverence, incorruptibility, sound speech that cannot be condemned, that one who is an opponent may be ashamed having nothing evil to say of you … denying ungodliness and worldly lusts, we should live soberly, righteously and godly in the present age. (Titus 2:2–12 NKJV)

Then this Daniel distinguished himself above the governors and satraps because an excellent spirit was in him; and the king gave thought to setting him over the whole realm. So the governors and satraps sought to find some charge against Daniel concerning the kingdom; but they could find no charge or fault, because he was faithful; nor was there any error or fault found in him. (Daniel 6:3–4 NKJV)

The righteousness of the blameless will direct his way aright, but the wicked will fall by his own wickedness. (Proverbs 11:5 NKJV)

Yet indeed I also count all things loss … and count them as rubbish, that I may gain Christ and be found in Him, not having my own righteousness, which is from the law, but that which is through faith in Christ, the righteousness which is from God by faith; that I may know Him and the power of His resurrection and the fellowship of His sufferings, being conformed to His death, if, by any means, I may attain to the resurrection from the dead. (Philippians 3:7–11 NKJV)

But whoever has this world's goods and sees his brother in need and shuts up his heart from him, how does the love of God abide in him? (1 John 3:17 NKJV)

## The Gospel Shoes

And having shod your feet with the preparation of the gospel of peace …
(Ephesians 6:15 NKJ)

The Word of God says your feet are beautiful if they are busy spreading the gospel of our Lord Jesus Christ. Feet working for the Lord have little time to get involved in mischief. The gospel shoes are part of God's armor. It stands for your initiative, eagerness, and zeal to do something for God. Servants of God should be eager to talk about what Jesus means to them and what he has done for them—to talk about who Christ is. It is not necessary to have the in-your-face approach. It can be subtle, simply dropping a few words about the Lord as often as the Holy Spirit gives you the opportunity. But you should have a heart and desire for it.

When people ask you what you believe and why, you should be prepared and excited to tell them. Share God's Word with them. What Scriptures would you want to tell them about first? If asked what the Bible says about a given topic, would you know? Would you be able to tell them where to look the answer up in the Bible? If you can't answer these questions, start spending more time in God's Word.

If you aren't reading and studying the Bible yourself, how can you share it with others? Perhaps you should ask yourself, "What am I doing to increase my understanding and knowledge of God and his word?" First

I would strongly encourage you to find a small group in your church that opens God's Word together. In addition, the Christian bookstores are full of great Bible studies, devotionals, and other resources for study on your own.

> Preach the word! Be ready in season and out of season. Convince, rebuke, exhort, with all longsuffering and teaching. (2 Timothy 4:2 NKJV)

> Be diligent to present yourself approved to God, a worker who does not need to be ashamed, rightly dividing the word of truth. (2 Timothy 2:15 NKJV)

> How beautiful upon the mountains are the feet of him who brings good news, who proclaims peace, who brings glad tidings of good things, who proclaims salvation, who says to Zion, "Your God reigns!" (Isaiah 52:7 NKJV)

> For though by this time you ought to be teachers, you need someone to teach you again the first principles of the oracles of God; and you have come to need milk and not solid food. For everyone who partakes only of milk is unskilled in the world of righteousness, for he is a babe. But solid food belongs to those who are of full age, that is, those who by reason of use have their senses exercised to discern both good and evil. (Hebrews 5:12–14 NKJV)

**The Faith Shield**

> Above all, taking the shield of faith with which you will be able to quench all the fiery darts of the wicked one. (Ephesians 6:16 NKJV)

Faith is a vital aspect of your daily Christian walk. There will be times that you simply do not understand why God is allowing you to go through something. We so often want to ask, "Why?" or "Why me?" There are definite times you will not be able to comprehend how God can make anything good out of your circumstances. Faith will see you through those gray and bleak times.

When your child comes to you crying because she is afraid and doesn't understand what's happening, you smile and reassure her. You say, "It's okay. Trust me. Everything will be fine." As the adult, you understand the situation, but since you know children's limited experience and undeveloped minds are incapable of understanding it, you don't bother explaining how it will all work out. You simply tell them to trust you, and you expect them to calm down (which they generally do). We are God's children. He is so much more capable than we are, that when he tells us in his word to trust him, we should be more like little children and calm down. Realize that you don't have to understand everything; just trust him. He has never failed you, but you must learn to obey Him in faith.

> So then faith comes from hearing, and hearing by the word of God. (Romans 10:17 NKJV)

> Now faith is the assurance of things hoped for, the conviction of things not seen. (Hebrews 11:1 ESV)

> Let us hold fast the confession of our hope without wavering, for He who promised is faithful. And let us consider how to stir up one another to love and good works, not neglecting to meet together as is the habit of some, but encouraging one another, and all the more as you see the Day drawing near. (Hebrews 10:23–25 ESV)

> Who shall separate us from the love of Christ? Shall tribulation, or distress, or persecution, or famine, or nakedness, or danger, or sword? … No, in all these things we are more than conquerors through him who loved us. For I am sure that neither death nor life, nor angels nor rulers, nor things present nor things to come, nor height nor depth, nor anything else in all creation, will be able to separate us from the love of God in Christ Jesus our Lord. (Romans 8:35, 37–39 ESV)

## The Helmet of Salvation

> And take the helmet of salvation …
> (Ephesians 6:17 NKJV)

Once you become a child of the king, you should do good works. However, don't be confused: doing good works does not save you. Salvation is a free gift of God through Jesus Christ. You cannot earn it. You don't deserve it; nobody does. That's why Jesus, God's only son, came to earth to die the horrid death by crucifixion. He, being perfect (something none of us can achieve), gave his life as a sacrifice to God for the remission of our sins. Through him (only through Jesus) we gain salvation and access to God himself.

I like to think of this "helmet" as being unshakable or even hardheaded, if you will, in my understanding of how or why I am saved. My salvation is not based on what other people think, what they tell me, or how I feel. My salvation is based solely on the completed work of Jesus on the cross and his resurrection from the dead, combined with true repentance—turning away from iniquity to wholeheartedly follow Jesus as my Lord—excited to serve Christ now and forevermore. I seek no excuse to continue sinning, and I earnestly desire not to sin, but when I do, I know Jesus stands ready to accept my repentant heart, and he forgives me freely. This "helmet" of understanding protects me from being carried away and confused by every wind of false doctrine that I may come across. Blessed assurance!

> That if you confess with your mouth the Lord Jesus and believe in your heart that God has raised Him from the dead, you will be saved. For with the heart one believes unto righteousness, and with the mouth confession is made unto salvation. For "whoever calls on the name of the LORD shall be saved." (Romans 10:9–10, 13 NKJV)

> If we say that we have no sin, we deceive ourselves and the truth is not in us. If we confess our sins, He is faithful and just to forgive us our sins and to cleanse us from all unrighteousness. If we say that we have not sinned,

we make Him a liar, and His word is not in us. (1 John 1:8–10 NKJV)

For by grace you have been saved through faith, and that not of yourselves; it is the gift of God, not of works, lest anyone should boast. (Ephesians 2:8–9 NKJV)

## The Sword of the Holy Spirit

And take … the sword of the Spirit, which is the Word of God …
(Ephesians 6:17 NKJV)

The Holy Spirit is part of the trinity of God (God the father, God the son, and God the Holy Spirit). Shortly before Jesus died on the cross, he promised he would send the Holy Spirit to help guide us so we would not be alone. God is always with us through his Spirit, the comforter.

The Holy Spirit, like a sword, cuts to the heart of the matter and doesn't get entangled in the outward appearance of things. This mighty sword of the Lord is able to cut chains asunder that humankind is unable to break. In my experience and opinion, the inner chains of addiction can only truly be broken by the Spirit of God. Other examples would be the bondage of worry, fear, depression, regret, anger, etc.

The Spirit of God also gives the believer spiritual wisdom to see straight through a lie and discover the truth. The Holy Spirit of God is a mighty weapon of spiritual warfare, yet it is too often the only weapon we are unwilling to unsheathe. When you put it to use, it not only discovers truth in others, it will first make clear to you, little by little over time, all of your own weaknesses and spiritual shortcomings. Perhaps that is why we don't like to use it. But if you are serious about spiritual warfare, you cannot ignore it. Pick it up! Unsheathe it! Let the Spirit do his work in you and through you!

Then Moses said to him, "Are you zealous for my sake? Oh, that all the Lord's people were prophets and that the Lord would put His Spirit upon them!" (Numbers 11:29 NKJV)

For the Word of God is alive and active, sharper than any two-edged sword, piercing to the division of soul and of spirit, of joints and of marrow, and discerning the thoughts and intentions of the heart. And no creature is hidden from his sight, but all are naked and exposed to the eyes of him to whom we must give account. (Hebrews 4:12–13 ESV)

And I will ask the Father, and he will give you another Helper, to be with you forever, even the Spirit of truth, whom the world cannot receive, because it neither sees Him nor knows Him. You know Him, for He dwells with you and will be in you. (John 14:16–17 ESV)

Now we have received, not the spirit of the world, but the Spirit who is from God, that we might know the things that have been freely given to us by God. These things we also speak, not in words which man's wisdom teaches but which the Holy Spirit teaches, comparing spiritual things with spiritual. But the natural man does not receive the things of the Spirit of God, for they are foolishness to him; nor can he know them, because they are spiritually discerned. (1 Corinthians 2:12–14 NKJV)

But the manifestation of the Spirit is given to each one for the profit of all; for to one is given the word of wisdom through the Spirit, to another the word of knowledge through the same Spirit, to another faith by the same Spirit, to another gifts of healings by the same Spirit, to another the working of miracles, to another prophecy to another discerning of spirits, to another different kinds of tongues, to another the interpretation of tongues. But one and the same Spirit works all these things, distributing to each one individually as He wills. (1 Corinthians 12:7–11 NKJV)

But you shall receive power when the Holy Spirit has come upon you; and you shall be witnesses to Me in Jerusalem, and in all Judea and Samaria, and to the ends of the earth. (Acts 1:8 NKJV)

## 3. Know the Enemy (Ephesians 6:12)

Our real enemy is not a human being, but as the Word tells us: "spiritual principalities, powers, rulers of darkness, and spiritual hosts of wickedness in the heavenly places" (Ephesians 6:12 NKJV). In short, Satan and his demons are the enemy. It's so easy for us Hoseas to forget that Gomer is not the one we need to fight. Our enemy is not the person made of flesh and blood. Gomer is not the enemy, simply a pawn in Satan's plan. Gomer is a spiritual victim.

So how well do you know the real enemy, Satan? It's important for any soldier involved in warfare to know as much about the enemy as possible—not to feel defeated but to gain power for victory, to plan effective strategy, and to join forces with other allies. What are the enemy's strengths and weaknesses? What can you expect from the enemy? As you seek to fill in the blanks below, you will learn what the Bible teaches us about the enemy, Satan. Take the time to read each Scripture in any translation you choose. Fill in the blank with your own word from what you understand the passage to mean. The answer is not necessarily an exact word found in the Scripture passage. Use the commentary I offer under each scripture to help you also.

Satan is strengthened when you _____ your reputation.
1 Timothy 3:7
Your spiritual reputation is important. When it gets tarnished, Satan is able to strengthen his forces and cause further damage to both Gomer and you, not to mention anyone else in your life.

Satan _____ the whole world.
Revelation 12:9; Acts 13:8–10
Satan is a crafty deceiver. He works from all angles at the same time. While he is convincing you that Gomer is hopeless and that Gomer doesn't even

really want to quit, he'll be working to convince Gomer that he may as well not even try, because nobody loves him anyway.

Satan desires our _____.
Matthew 4:8–10; Luke 4:6–8; 2 Thessalonians 2:3–4
Satan wants to be king, to be declared the almighty supreme one, to take God's place on the throne of heaven. He cannot do that, so the next best thing is to get our praise and adulation. He tried to get Jesus to bow before him. Jesus wouldn't do it, so now he wants as many humans as possible to kneel to his will and influence.

Satan appears to _____ for a time, but in the end God will _____. Luke 18:1-8; Matt. 25:1-46; Lamentations 1:3-9; Nahum 1:2-3; Psalm 37
Why God allows Satan time and opportunity to attack mankind is something we are unlikely to understand in this lifetime. Nevertheless, Satan sometimes seems to get the better of us: we turn the cheek; we watch evildoers prosper; we watch cheaters get ahead of us seemingly without consequence. Yet we know God will overcome. God will repay. God will judge.

Satan needs _____ to work in your life.
Ephesians 4:25–27; Daniel 6:3–9
Unless you allow Satan to get his foot in the door, he cannot do damage. Yes, Satan is powerful on this earth, but we are children of the Most High God. Satan only overcomes us when we give him room.

Satan works through _____ to add misery.
1 Samuel 1:6; Matthew 16:21–23; 2 Timothy 4:9–16
Someone says something that hurts our feelings. Someone cuts us off in traffic to make us angry. Allowing our emotions to be so easily disturbed is one way that we allow Satan to get his foot in the door. Satan loves to work his mischief behind the guise of a friend, relative, or even a perfect stranger. He'd rather you curse that other person than realize he's the real problem. Curse Satan directly, and put the true enemy in his place.

Animal name for those who do not follow Christ: _____

Matthew 25:32–33
Spiritually speaking, all people are either sheep or this other animal.

Satan is not a mortal—he is a _____.
Ephesians 6:12; 1 John 4:1–6
We cannot see Satan. He is not a human being to shoot or stab. We cannot fight him in our flesh, only by the Spirit of God that lives in us.

Satan can be _____.
James 4:7; Romans 12:21
We don't have to succumb to the wiles of Satan. We are able to hold Satan at bay using God's strength. Our flesh may be weak, but God, who lives in us, is always stronger than Satan.

Satan's objective is _____.
Job 2:4–6; 1 Peter 5:8–10
Satan is so crafty that he convinces men he wants them to be happy and prosperous while his real goal is quite the opposite. He plans nothing but pain and suffering for us.

Satan is the father of _____.
John 8:44
Satan cannot tell the truth. Any line he's feeding you is not to be believed. For example, when he says nobody loves you, and you're ugly and boring, you must recognize his deceit and resist believing the words he has planted in your mind.

Satan has lost the power over _____.
Hebrews 2:14–16
Jesus died on the cross, but when he rose from the dead three days later he took these keys away from Satan, and this aspect of life lost its sting.

Satan preys on the _____ in the Lord.
1 Timothy 3:6; 1 Peter 5:8
Just like a lion preys on the babies, the old and diseased, so too does Satan. He preys on the novice and the weak, expecting to defeat them.

In the parable of the sower, who does the bird represent? _____
Mark 4:4, 15

Where Satan spends much of his time (3 words) _____
_____ _____ Job 1:7
Satan knows his time to deceive mankind on this earth is limited. So he
spends the majority of his time here wreaking as much havoc as possible.

Satan _____ the Scriptures.
Matthew 4:3–10
Satan knows God's Word very well—well enough, in fact, to try to use it
out of context to confuse us. That's why we must study it for ourselves so
he can't twist God's Word or it's meaning around in our minds. He will
also try to tell you the Bible is too hard to understand. That is another lie—
Satan doesn't want you to know God's Word. Dig in! God will teach you.

Satan instigates _____.
John 13:2, 27
In a play, he would be called the villain for his wicked scheming.

Satan is our _____.
1 Peter 5:8
He is the opposite of an ally. He is on the other side, so anything you
get from him, though it may seem great at first (like fame or fortune), is
temporary at best and is designed to draw you away from God.

The spiritual battleground is (2 words): _____ _____.
Ephesians 6:12

Another word for the wiles of Satan: _____.
Ephesians 6:11

What the demons said before they were thrown to the pigs (three words):
_____ _____ _____
Mark 5:8–9
Satan does not work alone. When he was removed from heaven, many
angels fell with him. Satan is the commander in chief of this outlaw band.

Nevertheless, 2 Kings 6:16–17 tells us we always have more on God's side of the battle.

Jesus heals those who are _____ by Satan.
Acts 10:38; Isaiah 61:1–3

Satan _____ God's name.
Psalm 74:10

We, like Jesus, are _____ by Satan.
Matthew 4:1

Satan has a _____
2 Timothy 2:23–26
Satan's schemes are not haphazard. He works hard figuring out what he can do to us to make us fall away from God.

Ultimately, Satan is controlled by _____.
Job 1:6–12

Answers to fill-in-the-blank: damage, deceives, worship, win, triumph, room, others, goat, spirit, resisted, destruction, lies, death, young/weak, Satan, on the earth, distorts, evil, adversary, heavenly places, trickery, we are many, oppressed, blasphemes, tempted, plan, God.

# CHAPTER 14

# RIDING THE RELAPSE ROLLER COASTER

What the true proverb says has happened to them: "The dog returns to its own vomit, and the sow, after washing herself, returns to wallow in the mire." (2 Peter 2:22 ESV)

As a dog returns to its vomit, so a fool repeats his foolishness. (Proverbs 26:11 NLT)

Will Gomer relapse?

The answer is almost assuredly yes. The cravings are likely to win a few battles, but this doesn't mean Gomer has stopped fighting or that Gomer has lost the entire war. How bad the relapse will be depends on Gomer's reaction to it. Understanding relapse and even predicting it involves piecing together what we've learned so far.

**Chemical**: How long has Gomer been using? How much was used? Which drugs were used? Depending on these important factors, the brain chemistry could take several years to return to its natural balance once Gomer stays clean. This is a big reason why many addicts relapse after a year or two of sobriety. To you, it looks like Gomer is fully recovered. Gomer appears to be doing so well, and then, out of the blue Gomer disappears into his drug world. After fourteen months! After nineteen months! Exasperated, you ask, "How could Gomer do that?!" In Gomer's brain, the cells haven't recovered, so while Gomer appears healthy on the outside, he may still be healing on the inside.

**Psychological**: To what extent has Gomer dealt with his personal demons? Does Gomer still blame others, or has he started introspective healing? Has Gomer been able to openly and honestly discuss his past drug use with others besides you? Psychological scars are pesky and disruptive. Just when a person feels like he has gotten over a past hurt, it may resurface unexpectedly. The person may not be equipped to fight it and may not even try. He may feel totally defeated. Humans gain strength over emotional weakness partly by opening up to others. The more one willingly talks the less likely the emotional demons will cause Gomer to stumble. This, of course, takes years as well.

**Cultural**: Has Gomer's circle of friends changed? Does he spend less time in drug-receptive environments? Has his attitude toward drug use in general changed? Does Gomer openly rely on his new friends by calling on them when he's feeling low? This is another front on which to wage war. If Gomer hasn't changed friends and his attitude toward drug use is still, "Drugs are okay to use—I just need to cut back," then relapse is only a matter of time.

No matter how much resolve Gomer has to never use again, if he still spends much time with the old drug buddies and in the old stomping ground, the cravings can overtake him, and the opportunity will be right there under his nose, literally. If family members are drug users and Gomer is unable or unwilling to stop seeing them regularly, guide Gomer (if possible) to only visit them with you. For your own sanity, you must remember you are only attempting to guide Gomer. Gomer will make the ultimate decision.

Holidays can also be a relapse-threatening time for Gomer. If Gomer has always used drugs on the holidays, then it's part of his tradition (warped as that may sound). The holidays will seem to be missing something to Gomer. He may not even realize what it is. The holidays are times to visit old friends and family, too. So even if Gomer's not been hanging out with the old gang, Gomer is likely to see them around the holidays. Remember Gomer perhaps still loves his old friends. Just because he knows he can't hang with the drugs anymore, the love for his friends doesn't simply die away. Drug buddies are sometimes *very* tight, almost like soldiers who have served together, especially if they have a long history.

**Spiritual**: Has Gomer accepted Jesus as his personal Savior? Does he regularly/daily spend time in Bible study and prayer? Is he hungry for spiritual growth and truth? Is he open to spiritual change and reproof? When he falls, does he quickly admit to the sin, ask for forgiveness, get up, and go on? Spiritual strength is the best deterrent to relapse. Even if Gomer has been saved and is steadily growing in God, that does not make him exempt from relapse. Surely there are sins that you and I struggle with, even though we have been saved. Perhaps it's gossiping, lying, being proud, or being judgmental. You ask God to forgive you, and you really mean it. God forgives. You do well for a while, but then one day you catch yourself. You again repent. The big difference is your sin may not be as socially visible or seemingly as personally damaging. But spiritually speaking, there is no difference. We all struggle with one sin or another.

We each learn to overcome our sinful nature as we draw closer to our Lord, but it doesn't happen overnight. Even Paul, who wrote a large part of the New Testament, grappled with a "thorn in the flesh" (2 Corinthians 12:7) that he never felt he could overcome. Whatever this thorn was, God never took it from him, but as he grew in Christ, he discovered Jesus' strength would see him through it. Give Gomer time to mature in Christ. Periodic relapse isn't the end of the road. How Gomer reacts to his own relapse each time will determine the degree of the damage.

**Enabling**: To what extent do you and others still enable Gomer? Is Gomer financially accountable for himself, or is he still dependent on others? Once a person has sobered up, enabling plays a smaller role. If Gomer relapses, I would not say that enabling was to blame—it's always Gomer's choice—however, it seems enabling can make it somewhat easier for Gomer to return to old drug patterns. When our loved one is in recovery, it's easy for a Hosea to once again fall into a pattern of enabling. This occurs for several reasons. We want to reward Gomer for quitting drugs; we believe we are reinforcing the sobriety; and we relax, thinking tough love is no longer needed.

So, what should *you* be doing during a relapse?

1.  Return to full spiritual warfare! It is so easy during recovery to relax, spiritually speaking—we stop fighting the spiritual enemy. Keep waging that war, because the enemy is only waiting for you to allow him to enter your camp once again. He hasn't given up forever on either you or Gomer. He will never completely go away. Review chapter 13.

2.  Check yourself. Make sure you are not claiming any blame. Gomer is solely responsible for relapse, just like he was responsible for getting hooked on drugs to begin with. Review chapter 4.

3.  Make sure you have not allowed your finances to mingle back together with Gomer's finances. If you have, immediately take the steps to separate your money once again. Review chapter 6.

4.  Check yourself that you have not returned to enabling Gomer in any way. Encourage others whenever possible to check themselves so no one (hopefully) is enabling Gomer. Review chapter 5.

5.  Consider again how you are currently communicating with Gomer. Remember you couldn't argue or reason Gomer into sobriety the first time, so you can't win the war of words this time either. Review chapter 3.

6.  If Gomer quickly gets back on track, be thankful, and be careful not to harbor ill feelings and hurts. Chalk it up as a slip in the mud. Watch, too, that the slips do not occur frequently and do not form a pattern (such as once a month, every long weekend, or every time certain people come around). If a pattern begins to form, it's a sign that Gomer is trying to have the best of both worlds: a loving Hosea to nurture and love him, *and* the drugs on a regular basis. Full-blown relapse is never far away from this pattern (or perhaps he never really quit?).

7.  If Gomer doesn't quickly get back on track you'll need to reassess your situation and pray. The Lord will help you decide with peace of mind what to do. Jesus will help you make both small decisions, such as what to say to Gomer that might encourage him to return to sobriety, and big decisions, such as whether or not you need to separate for your own mental health and financial security.

8.  Remember the rules of reaping follow relapse, too. Be prepared to watch Gomer face consequences once again. This can be extremely

painful. Maybe all the old bills are on the verge of getting paid off for the first time in years. Maybe Gomer finally found a good job and was doing very well at work. But now in the midst of relapse Gomer is facing unemployment, and bills are mounting up once again! It's maddening! If you've been faithful to God, the rules of reaping will apply to you as well for the good … remember? There are good rules, too. God is perfectly capable of allowing Gomer to face his consequences while giving you a time of prosperity (Isaiah 65:13–14). You will not personally go without as long as you are faithful (assuming you don't waste your blessings by enabling Gomer further—handing over your finances to Gomer once again). Review chapter 2.

9. Be prepared to forgive—yes, again! Even if you choose to leave Gomer, it's important for your own emotional health and spiritual well-being to forgive (Matthew 18:21–35). God commands his children to forgive, and he gives us the heart to do so. Review chapter 9.

10. Get counseling from a spiritual leader who has experience with addiction, and/or go to group support meetings available in your area. Sharing your pain with others who understand can be healing. Also, knowing you are not the first or last to go through this kind of pain is comforting. I do advise, however, that you compare their advice with what the Bible says. Although others may be going through a situation like yours, their advice may not be godly or even good. Moreover, what "worked" in their situation isn't guaranteed to "work" for you. Listen to others, and then filter all their ideas and comments through prayer and God's Word.

11. Most of all, remember to keep your stability, peace of mind, and self-esteem founded on the rock of Jesus Christ—*never* on Gomer. Whether Gomer is in recovery or relapse, he is *not* where you store peace, stability, or self-esteem. Review chapters 7, 8, and 10 when you feel loneliness lurking in the shadows or your peace of mind drifting away from you in the outgoing tide.

# CHAPTER 15

# SO YOU'RE READY TO WALK AWAY?

There is no human cure for addiction. No one can say with certainty when or even if your Gomer will ever give up his drug of choice. Although Christ is able to heal all diseases, he is a gentleman and never forces his will on mankind.

> Behold my servant, whom I uphold, my chosen, in whom my soul delights; I have put my Spirit upon him; he will bring forth justice to the nations. He will not cry aloud or lift up his voice, or make it heard in the street; a bruised reed he will not break, and a faintly burning wick he will not quench. (Isaiah 42:1–3 ESV)

> I call heaven and earth as witnesses today against you, that I have set before you life and death, blessing and cursing; therefore choose life, that both you and your descendants may live. (Deuteronomy 30:19 NKJJV)

Life is a series of choices. Receiving help from God is also a choice. Gomer may never choose to deal with his addictions and therefore may never overcome his problems, even though Jesus is right there and wants to help him. Of course, you must also choose God's help. He won't force himself on you either.

When I called you did not answer; when I spoke you did not hear, but did evil before My eyes and chose that in which I do not delight. (Isaiah 65:12 NKJV)

Now I'm not trying to cause you to lose hope. Hope through Christ eternal and pray for Gomer always! Yet practically speaking, you may not always be able or willing to live with the addict.

And if it seems evil to you to serve the Lord, choose for yourselves this day whom you will serve … but as for me and my house, we will serve the Lord. (Joshua 24:15 NKJV)

Go from the presence of a foolish man when you do not perceive in him the lips of knowledge. The wisdom of the prudent is to understand his way, but the folly of fools is deceit. Fools mock at sin, but among the upright there is favor. (Proverbs 14:7–9 NKJV)

Drive out a scoffer, and strife will go out, and quarreling and abuse will cease. (Proverbs 22:10 ESV)

**There are practical reasons for leaving:**

- Physical abuse
- Emotional abuse
- Financial ruin (facing poverty/homelessness due to addiction spending)
- Your own emotional ruin (suicidal thoughts and tendencies)

I cannot tell you whether you should separate from Gomer. No one can tell you when to leave or if you should get back together (although many will try). You alone can make these decisions. I strongly suggest much prayer before making such decisions. Note: if your Gomer is your spouse, I haven't used the word "divorce." I personally do not endorse divorce; yet neither do I judge you for divorcing. I am not saying here you must completely wash your hands of him or never see him again. However,

I recognize that there may come a time that you need to live apart from Gomer. These are your decisions to make with God based on your personal circumstances.

I do not recommend you leave Gomer as an emotional ploy, an attempt to make him see the error of his ways, thinking, "I'll show him!" Leaving him needs to be a real weighed-out decision, one that his usual promises of change won't immediately or easily alter. It needs to be a decision that won't fade away two weeks later, when Gomer appears to be cleaning up, and send you back at Gomer's whim. Your decision to leave should ultimately bring you spiritual and emotional healing and peace, rather than continued turmoil. The same goes for when or if you decide to live with Gomer again after a period of separation. The decision to reunite should be equally weighed out and prayed over.

So if you do decide to separate, do you leave, or do you make Gomer leave? Do you lock Gomer out? What should you do with his belongings? I believe the Lord would not want you to act out of anger, for instance, by throwing Gomer's things out in the yard or destroying or selling them. There are Christian ways to handle Gomer's property. Box it up and store it, or give it to someone Gomer will be seeing (like his mother or a friend). You may choose to keep it at your own home in storage until he comes to get it.

If Gomer's your spouse, it's more complex. You both may want or need to keep certain items, such as TV, computers, etc. If Gomer won't discuss it with you rationally, or won't be reasonable, or just hasn't come home (out on a drug binge?), then be generous and thoughtful toward Gomer when you select what to keep for yourself. God will honor you for it and bless you in the long run. Even so, Gomer may not recognize your generosity. It's more likely Gomer will remain *very* hard to deal with and unfair toward you. You should expect this.

Remember, Gomer may be so totally engrossed in his drugs and the drug culture that he is simply *not* capable of making logical decisions. The entire load may rest on your shoulders. Pray, meditate on God, and do your best. Do not carry guilt over having to make these decisions. The decisions had to be made! Gomer's irresponsibility forced your hand. So release yourself from guilt and shame. Remember? It's not about you.

When I finally separated from my husband after several years of living on the drug roller coaster, we were living in near poverty in an old broken-down mobile home. There was little food to eat. The electricity and cable were a couple days away from being disconnected for nonpayment. I knew my next small paycheck would give me enough money to pay these bills or to move out—not both. I had been praying all summer over what I should do. Each month, I didn't feel like God wanted me to go—not quite yet. Then, in October, my husband forced my hand, and I knew God was giving me the yes I had been waiting for. I moved out, and God provided everything I needed. I was very careful with my money and didn't have much left over, but I didn't go without anything I truly needed either. God is faithful.

When Gomer realizes you are really separating (or kicking him out as the case may be), an emotional barrage will begin. Up until now, Gomer has been able to continue with perhaps only a few real consequences; and when you've talked of leaving (and I know you have), Gomer made a few promises to change, or he played the sympathy card. Perhaps he even mentioned suicide. Whatever emotion Gomer used in the past—it worked! You stayed; you let him stay. But now, as Gomer is facing actual separation, he is going to use each emotion, one by one, hoping one of them will work and cause you to stay (or allow him to stay). He probably doesn't realize he is doing this, but you should expect it.

Remember the response you should use? "I'm sorry you feel that way." Don't allow Gomer to draw you back into the web of guilt or shame. Don't be afraid. You need not defend your decisions to Gomer. There is no reason to argue or fight about it. Tell Gomer you love him, and you'll be praying for him. He'll probably call you a liar (emotional ploy). After all, if you really loved him, he'll say, you'd stay and help him now that he's really going to quit. This will be Gomer's logic. It's reminiscent of taking something away from a spoiled child and hearing the child throw a fit while screaming, "I hate you!" Let Gomer throw his fit and say whatever he wants. Let it all slide off your back into the stream of God's eternal grace.

Be prepared to do what it takes for your safety. You know your special circumstances better than I do. My husband was never violent or abusive toward me, so I was able to safely leave with two girlfriends, who helped me to move out. I was even able to take a carload of possessions with me. Your situation could play out very differently. Honestly consider your Gomer's past actions and your present situation. If he has *ever* slapped or struck you in any fashion, even once, or threatened to do so, he *is* capable of hurting you when you try to leave. Don't lie to yourself and say he wouldn't do that.

Consider the following safety tips:

- ➢ Involve other family members *only* if their involvement is likely to be a help to you. Only you know your family members well enough to know if they will be a help or a hindrance in this situation. Sometimes just the presence of a big brother is enough to keep Gomer from becoming violent. Other times, family members may only make the scene worse by escalating the fighting and adding to your stress.
- ➢ You could choose to have friends help you. You need their muscles for loading the car or to pack up his belongings anyway. There is safety in numbers, and they can serve as your witnesses if needed. Use the same rule for choosing friends as you used for choosing family members.
- ➢ Involve the police or the courts. If Gomer has been violent in the past or has *any* tendency toward physical abuse, then get an order of protection before you attempt to move out or move him out. The police can only protect you if the order of protection is in place first. If Gomer gets abusive when you are trying to move out or trying to kick him out, then call the police. Without the order of protection in place the police have power merely to break up a fight. Of course an order of protection is really only a piece of paper—Gomer may choose to ignore it, but that paper is still worth having. Abuse and potential for abuse needs to be documented with the courts and police.
- ➢ Talk to an attorney if you have legal separation or financial concerns. Many attorneys offer a one-time free consultation. Listen to their advice, and then pray. God will guide you. You may also find free legal aid available in your area. Ask around.

Whether you are the one moving out or you are forcing Gomer to leave, there are a number of things to consider. Do not be overwhelmed by this list. Mark what applies to you, and then check things off as you pray and make your decisions.

1. Where will you live, if you are the one moving out?

- With a family member?
- With friends?
- Go to a shelter at first?
- Rent your own apartment, house, or trailer?
- Rent low-income housing? (It can take months to get into a unit.)
- Rent a room in someone else's home? (Ask a pastor if he knows of a room for rent. This worked for me.)
- What kind of lease are you willing to sign? Three, six, or twelve months?
- Can your pets live in your new place? If not, do you know someone who will keep them for you temporarily? Will you need to find a new permanent home for them?

2. Financial considerations.

- Reread chapter 6, Financial Accountability.
- Do you have any savings or other funds available to you?
- What kind of moving expenses can you handle? (Consider U-Haul, gas, utility hookup fees, deposits, lost wages for time off work while moving, etc.)
- List what you expect your monthly expenses will be (rent, electric, water, cable, telephone, car payments, car insurance, health insurance, etc.) and plan a tentative budget based solely on your income. Do *not* include *any* money in your budget that is meant to come from Gomer, even if it's court ordered. Do not rely on Gomer. If Gomer gives it to you, it is extra money to go into savings or to more quickly pay down debt. But if you depend on it and then it doesn't come, you are the one who can't pay rent! You can be mad all you want but your rent will still not be paid!

- List any variable expenses you can think of (food, gasoline, car repair, birthday gifts, etc.).
- Separate your bank accounts if you haven't already done so. Get the bank accounts in your name only. Don't ask Gomer to remove his name from the joint account! Don't tell him you are doing this. Simply start up your own account in your name. You may wish to tell your bank the reason for establishing your own account so they can notify you should Gomer try to withdraw cash from your new account.

I never thought my husband would do this, and furthermore, I never thought the bank would allow it. But my husband (who is very charming) managed to forge my checks for cash at the bank while I was out of town and spent all my money and five hundred dollars more. The bank told me that unless I was willing to charge my husband with forgery at the police station, the bank had no obligation to replace my money! I wasn't willing. The money was gone. My account was five hundred dollars in the negative, and I had to find a way to pay it back. That was my angle for not charging my husband with forgery: I told him as long as he paid the bank the five hundred dollars and covered every dead check with all associated fees before they went to court, I would not charge him with forgery. But should even *one* bad check come back on me, then I would have gone to the police immediately! I wasn't bluffing and he knew it! He diligently covered every last check very quickly. I don't know where the money came from. I didn't care at the time. I didn't ask.

- List any past due bills in your name.
- Consider credit counseling.
- Should you get a second job? Should you change jobs? Can you work overtime at your current job for added income?
- Are there any monthly bills you can trim down? For example: if you have movie channels on your cable bills, cancel the movie

portion. Or if you have Internet access—unless you work online as a source of income, cancel the Internet until your finances can afford it. Think of other ways to trim your expenditures.

3. Other considerations if you make Gomer leave.

- Get the locks changed. Even if Gomer gave you the keys, he could still have duplicates.
- Take back Gomer's set of keys to your vehicles.
- Work with bill collectors to ward off electricity disconnections, etc. Don't ignore them. They will work with you, especially if you explain what's been going on and the changes you have just made.
- Are there any monthly bills you can trim down? For example: if you have movie channels on your cable bills, cancel the movie portion. Or if you have Internet access—unless you work online as a source of income, cancel the Internet until your finances can afford it. Think of other ways to trim your expenditures.

4. Other considerations.

- Are your kids going to be changing schools?
- Who will provide child care after the move?
- Change your address at the post office. Inform friends, relatives, and companies of your new address and other contact information that has changed.
- Do you want or need to change beneficiaries on life insurance policies?
- Do you want or need to change health insurance benefits to exclude Gomer?
- Do you need or want to make any changes to your social media? For example, does Gomer have your Facebook password? Twitter account? You may want to unfriend or block Gomer and others from your social media, too. Do not be aggravated daily by their posts about you or what Gomer is doing now.
- Do you need or want to change your cell phone number?

If Gomer really does use his time apart from you to clean up (for real), then his sobriety is likely to last, even when you don't return to him immediately, even if you don't return at all. Gomer's sobriety will only last if he has cleaned up for himself, not just to get you to return to him. I recommend you stay separated for at least six months to a year. Then, if he's still clean, working, and implementing more constructive ways to deal with problems in general, then pray to God about whether or not to get back together.

During the separation, if Gomer is your spouse, you may choose to date each other so you don't drift apart. You should make dating rules and stick to them. For example, because I knew my husband was great at coming up with excuses (aren't all addicts experts at this?), one rule I made was that if he was even one minute late to pick me up for our date, I would not go with him. No excuses. Either I'm worth it to you, or I'm not really a priority. He was only five minutes late one time, and I refused to go. Another example: every Sunday there was an addiction meeting (AA style), which I also attended. We were living about an hour apart, and the meeting was about halfway for both of us. The rule was if he didn't come, or if he came but was in my view not participating and being honest, then I would not see him or talk with him by phone at all during the coming week. If he came to the next meeting, then we could talk and see each other that week. He only missed one meeting, and when he tried to call me that week, I only answered long enough to say, "See you at the next meeting. I'll talk to you then." And I hung up.

He knew my rules were strict, and I would stick to them. We dated like this for more than six months. We went to marriage counseling a couple of times during this period, too. When Lonnie wanted me to move back in with him, I made the rule that I would when and if he found a new place for us and paid for rent, deposits, and other fees all by himself. I knew he could only do that if he stayed clean and I didn't really expect it to happen. It took him a couple months to accomplish this; then I did move back in with him in keeping my word. He stayed clean one year, and then I found myself rereading this book (in its unpublished form) as he relapsed. It was almost another year of misery before he took his last hit. But this time, I followed the concepts of this book very closely. I didn't fall apart to the extreme that I had before. It was not easy or fun, but God did see me through it. Praise God! What a testimony now!

My rules were about *my* serenity; they were not about punishing him or trying to control him. The rules protected me. When he stayed clean, my rules were never a problem. If he didn't stay clean, then the rules protected me from the garbage his addiction carried around. You will make decisions that work for you. Pray about them. Think them through. Make peace with them. Change your rules, or add to the rules only as needed, but not too often. Gomer needs to know the areas in which you are simply unmovable. You need to know your boundaries are secure too!

# CHAPTER 16

# DON'T LOSE OUT

Do you love Jesus? Really. It's a serious question. Do you love him? Peter was asked that same question three times by Jesus himself in John 21:15–19. Why would Jesus repeatedly ask Peter the same question? Was Peter lying when he answered yes? I don't believe so. Peter did love the Lord Jesus, yet the Lord knew Peter's future of struggle, imprisonment, and death by crucifixion. Peter needed to know within himself that he loved the Lord, that regardless of life's situations he would continue steadfastly to serve the Lord from this point forward, to never deny him again.

So I ask you the third time: do you love Jesus? Will you allow the trials of life to turn you bitter inside and cause you to leave the faith? What if Gomer never cleans up? Will you get angry with God for that and stop serving him? What if Gomer dies from suicide or overdose? Will that separate you from God? What if you never find fame or fortune? What if you are paralyzed in an accident? What if you go blind? What if your best friend is brutally raped and murdered? What if your child dies tragically?

I'm not trying to be morbid. Reality can be cold. We need to determine within ourselves that our love for God is not based on good circumstances. The apostle Paul grappled with this very question. Is there anything that can separate me from God's love?

> For I am persuaded that neither death nor life, nor angels
> nor principalities nor powers not things present nor things
> to come, nor height nor depth, nor any other created thing

shall be able to separate us from the love of God which is in Christ Jesus our Lord. (Romans 8:38–39 NKJV)

You are the only one who can separate you from God. God will not pull away from you, but he won't prevent you from ultimately walking away from him. Our choices, our sins, separate us from God. He has the rules of reaping in place, so hopefully you will see the error of your ways and return to him. The Scriptures are full of admonishments that we should remain faithful to God, and they warn us of common pitfalls along the Christian road.

Therefore, as the Holy Spirit says: "Today, if you will hear His voice, do not harden your hearts as in the rebellion, in the day of trial in the wilderness, where your fathers tested Me, tried Me, And saw My works forty years." … For we have become partakers of Christ if we hold the beginning of our confidence steadfast to the end. (Hebrews 3:7–14 NKJV)

Therefore do not cast away your confidence, which has great reward. For you have need of endurance so that after you have done the will of God, you may receive the promise: "For yet a little while, and He who is coming will come and will not tarry. Now the just shall live by faith; but if anyone draws back, My soul has no pleasure in him." But we are not of those who draw back to perdition, but of those who believe to the saving of the soul. (Hebrews 10:35–39 NKJV)

Therefore strengthen the hands which hang down and the feeble knees, and make straight paths for your feet, so that what is lame may not be dislocated, but rather be healed. Pursue peace with all people and holiness, without which no one will see the Lord: looking carefully lest anyone fall short of the grace of God; lest any root of bitterness springing up cause trouble, and by this many become defiled. (Hebrews 12:12–15 NKJVJ)

Do your best to present yourself to God as one approved, a worker who has no need to be ashamed, rightly handling the word of truth. (2 Timothy 2:15 ESV)

Therefore, beloved, looking forward to these things, be diligent to be found in Him in peace, without spot and blameless and consider that the longsuffering of our Lord is salvation ... You therefore, beloved, since you know this beforehand, beware lest you also fall from your own steadfastness, being led away with the error of the wicked; but grow in grace and knowledge of our Lord and Savior Jesus Christ. (2 Peter 3:14–15, 17–18 NKJV)

But also for this very reason giving all diligence, add to your faith virtue, to virtue knowledge, to knowledge self-control, to self-control perseverance, to perseverance godliness, to godliness brotherly kindness, and to brotherly kindness love. For if these things are yours and abound, you will be neither barren nor unfruitful in the knowledge of our Lord Jesus Christ. For he who lacks these things is shortsighted, even to blindness, and has forgotten that he was cleansed from his old sins. Therefore, brethren, be even more diligent to make your call and election sure, for if you do these things you will never stumble; for so an entrance will be supplied to you abundantly into the everlasting kingdom of our Lord and Savior Jesus Christ. (2 Peter 1:5–11 NKJV)

Everyone who goes on ahead and does not abide in the teaching of Christ, does not have God. (2 John 1:9 ESV)

Only fear the Lord and serve Him faithfully with all your heart. For consider what great things He has done for you. (1 Samuel 12:24 ESV)

"For My people have committed two evils: They have forsaken Me, the fountain of living waters, And hewn themselves cisterns—broken cisterns that can hold no water. Your own wickedness will correct you, And your backslidings will rebuke you. Know therefore and see that it is an evil and bitter thing that you have forsaken the LORD your God, and the fear of Me is not in you," says the Lord GOD of hosts. "For of old I have broken your yoke and burst your bonds; and you said, 'I will not transgress.' ... How then have you turned before Me into the degenerate plant of an alien vine?" (Jeremiah 2:13, 19–21 NKJV)

"As for you, my son Solomon, know the God of your father, and serve Him with a loyal heart and with a willing mind; for the Lord searches all hearts and understands all the intent of the thoughts. If you seek Him, He will be found by you; but if you forsake Him, He will cast you off forever. (1 Chronicles 28:9 NKJV)

It is vital that as a lover of the Lord you have personal endurance in Christ. I like to call it Christian grit—a raw determination to serve the Lord with all your heart, soul, and body. It's this strong, deep-rooted love for Christ that gives you the ability to praise him and laugh in the face of a storm; to smile at the one who mocks you for your beliefs; and to pray for the one who tries to harm you. It's that same grit that keeps you working in the ministry in the face of criticism. Your faith in Jesus Christ cannot be based on the opinions of others or on the circumstances of life. Rather, your belief must be unshakably based upon the Word of God. That way, you will remain stable, unwavering, and spiritually unconquerable!

For what if some did not believe? Will their unbelief make the faithfulness of God without effect? Certainly not! (Romans 3:3–4 NKJV)

I pray that you will find that Christian grit and hold on to your faith with the same tenacity a football player uses to hold onto the football as he races to the end zone with the opposition close at his heels. I wish I could tell you that Gomer will defeat the drugs, clean up, and live a wonderful, prosperous Christian life with you. I wish I could tell you it will be easy. I wish I could tell you that relapse won't happen, and the worst is now over. Of course, I cannot say any of those things; they are unknown at this time and will unfold in the future. I can only personally tell you that regardless of what your Gomer does, *you* can have a happy, prosperous life for yourself in the Lord. My prayers are with you always.

> And the Spirit and the bride say, Come.
> And let him that heareth say, Come.
> And let him that is athirst come.
> And whosoever will, let him take the water of life freely.
> (Revelation 22:17 KJV)

# MY PLAYLIST

I find music a powerful tool. God has always used music as one way to speak to me. In the Bible we learn David was a man after God's own heart, and David loved music! The Book of Psalms is a collection of songs. Most of the recorded psalms were written by David, and they were meant to cause one to reflect, remember, and worship. Like the songs of David, modern Christian music often teaches us through their lyrics about God's Word. These contemporary lyrics serve to encourage, strengthen, and uplift a weary traveler. The songs I have selected have lyrics that move me. I must say, however, I do not know any of these artists personally. Having listed an artist in this appendix does not mean I endorse their personal beliefs, views, or life choices.

Many songs have come to my mind as I edited this book. I also searched and found new music to enjoy, which I have included here. Since I enjoy a wide variety of musical styles, below you will find a combination of contemporary Christian, Christian rock, gospel, southern gospel, and alternative Christian songs on my playlist. The words of each song selected are strongly connected to the writings of this book. I pray they bless you as they have me, time and time again!

To create your own musical library, look these songs/artists up on the Internet, through iTunes, or ask your favorite music store to help you locate them. I searched iTunes under the genre "Christian & Gospel." Many more songs could be added, and I'm sure you probably have your own list of Christian songs that move you. Connect your songs to the messages found in this book, and create for yourself a resource of music that moves you in your time of need.

Turn up the volume, soak up the sounds, and sing out loud!

Chapter 1: Why Is It So Hard to Quit?
"All You've Ever Wanted" by Casting Crowns
"The Altar and the Door" by Casting Crowns
"Always Have, Always Will" by Avalon
"Avalanche" by Manafest
"Awake My Soul" by Chris Tomlin
"Between You and Me" by DC Talk
"Blind" by Third Day
"Christ Is Able" by Charles Billingsley
"Come Ye Sinners" by Todd Agnew
"Dive" by DC Talk
"I Need a Miracle" by Third Day
"I've Come to Take You Home" by The Isaacs
"Mighty to Save" by Hillsong
"The One I'm Dying For" by The Isaacs
"Peace" by The Isaacs
"People Like Me" by Mikeschair
"Reached Down" by Todd Agnew
"Remedy" by Disciple
"Romans" by Jennifer Knapp
"Save Your Life" by Newsboys
"Sinner's Prayer" by Deitrick Haddon
"Someone Searching" by Ginny Owens
"Stained Glass Masquerade" by Casting Crowns
"Wait for Your Rain" by Todd Agnew
"The Well" by Casting Crowns
"When Mercy Found Me" by Rhett Walker Band

Chapter 2: Rules of Reaping
"As It Is in Heaven" by Matt Maher
"Between the Cross and Crown" by NewSong
"Calling Out to You" by Maranatha! Promise Band

140

"The Change" by Steven Curtis Chapman
"Come One, Come All" by MercyMe
"Great Expectations" by Steven Curtis Chapman
"If My People Pray" by Avalon
"The Invitation" by Steven Curtis Chapman
"Jesus My Lord, My God, My All" by Maranatha! Promise Band
"Pray" by Darlene Zschech
"Refine Me" by Jennifer Knapp
"Show Me Your Glory" by Third Day
"Take You at Your Word" by Avalon
"This Beating Heart" by Matt Redman
"Untitled Hymn (Come to Jesus)" by Chris Tomlin
"White Flag" by Passion
"Wholly Yours" by David Crowder Band

Chapter 3: Communication Guidelines
"Be Still and Know" by Steven Curtis Chapman
"The Change Inside of Me" by MercyMe
"Fence Riders" by Jimmy Needham
"In the Light" by DC Talk
"Jesus Mighty Fortress" by Maranatha! Promise Band
"Learning to Be the Light" by NewWorldSon
"Not My Will" by Maranatha! Promise Band
"Only for the Weak" by Avalon
"Only One Thing" by Todd Agnew
"Speechless" by Steven Curtis Chapman
"This Fragile Breath" by Todd Agnew
"The Word of God Has Spoken" by Travis Cottrell
"Word of God Speak" by MercyMe
"The Words I Would Say" by Sidewalk Prophets

Chapter 4: Don't Claim the Blame
"Blind" by Third Day
"Christ Is Able" by Charles Billingsley
"Dear X, You Don't Own Me" by Disciple
"Give Me Your Eyes" by Brandon Heath

"Grace Like Rain" by Todd Agnew
"I'm Changed" by Travis Cottrell
"Jesus in a Song" by The Crabb Family
"Lay 'Em Down" by Needtobreathe
"Lay It Down" by Todd Agnew
"Letting Go" by Bethel Music
"Still" by Hillsong
"Washed by the Water" by Needtobreathe
"Your Great Name" by Natalie Grant
"Your Name" by Maranatha! Promise Band

Chapter 5: Stop Enabling
"Break Every Chain" by The Digital Age
"Cornerstone" (featuring Audrey Assad) by Tim Neufeld
"Cry Out to Jesus" by Third Day
"Every Now and Then" by FFH
"Free" by Hillsong
"Gravity" by Shawn McDonald
"I'm Not Who I Was" by Brandon Heath
"Jesus Will Do What You Can't" by The Crabb Family
"Just Might Change Your Life" by Sidewalk Prophets
"Let Go" by BarlowGirl
"New Season" by Israel Houghton & New Breed
"O My Soul, March On" by Travis Cottrell
"Pure" by Superchick
"Something Beautiful" by Needtobreathe
"Stand Still" by The Isaacs
"Walk by Faith" by Jeremy Camp
"We Will Stand" by Maranatha! Promise Band
"Whatever It Takes" by Nate Sallie
"You Are God Alone" by Marvin Sapp

Chapter 6: Financial Accountability
"Broken Man" by Rhett Walker Band
"Dive" by Steven Curtis Chapman
"Everything I Need" by Kutless

"Hear Us from Heaven" by New Life Worship
"Hide My Soul" by Avalon
"I Am Resting" by Tricia Brock
"In The Name" by Jennifer Knapp
"Jesus Mighty Fortress" by Maranatha! Promise Band
"Mountain of God" by Third Day
"Ready for You" by Kutless
"Unspoken" by Jaci Velasquez
"Why Worry" by NewSong
"Window" by Out of Eden
"You Are" by Colton Dixon
"You Are for Me" by Kari Jobe
"You Are Good" by Maranatha! Promise Band
"Your Latter Will Be Greater" by Israel Houghton & New Breed

Chapter 7: Overcoming Loneliness and Low Self-Esteem
"All Things New" by Sidewalk Prophets
"Born Again" by Third Day
"Eternal Wonderful God" by Maranatha! Promise Band
"Fingerprints of God" by Steven Curtis Chapman
"Forever" by Overflow
"Free" by Ginny Owens
"Friend 'Til the End" by The Isaacs
"Gold" by Britt Nicole
"Hide" by Joy Williams
"How Great Is Your Love" by Maranatha! Promise Band
"How He Loves" by John Mark McMillan
"I Bring It to You" by The Isaacs
"I Shall Not Want" by Audrey Assad
"I'm Changed" by Travis Cottrell
"I'm Going Free (Jailbreak)" by Vertical Church Band
"Leaving 99" by Audio Adrenaline
"More" by Matthew West
"Not Alone" by Red
"Ready to Fly" by FFH
"Right Here" by Jeremy Camp

"You Revive Me" (featuring Christy Nockels) by Passion
"You, You Are God" by Gateway Worship

Chapter 9: Learning to Forgive
"Between You and Me" by DC Talk
"Dear God" by The Martins
"Don't Deserve You" by Plumb
"Forgiveness" by Matthew West
"From the Inside Out" by Hillsong United
"Here I Am to Worship" by Maranatha! Promise Band
"His Grace is Sufficient" by Jennifer Knapp
"I Am Nothing" by Ginny Owens
"I Want to Be Like You" by FFH
"Kindness" by Todd Agnew
"Mercy" by Matt Redman
"More Like Falling in Love" by Jason Gray
"No Chains on Me" by Chris Tomlin
"Not Guilty" by Mandisa
"Nothing but the Blood" by Matt Redman
"Ocean Floor" by Audio Adrenaline
"Ocean Wide" by The Afters
"Own Me" by Ginny Owens
"Please Forgive Me" by the Crabb Family
"The Reason" by NewSong
"Redeemed" by Big Daddy Weave
"Should've Been Me" by Citizen Way
"Song of Freedom" by Hillsong
"Take My Life (Holiness)" by Micah Stampley
"That's How You Forgive" by Shane & Shane
"Todo Lo Puedo en Cristo" by Maranatha! Promise Band
"Undo Me" by Jennifer Knapp
"Unlike Me, Just Like Him" by The Isaacs
"What Mercy Means" by The Martins
"Whole Again" by Jennifer Knapp
"The Wonderful Cross" by Maranatha! Promise Band
"You Are My King (Amazing Love)" by Newsboys

"You Can Have Me" by Sidewalk Prophets
"You Love Me Anyway" by Sidewalk Prophets

Chapter 10: Holding On to Hope
    "Be My Glory" by FFH
    "From the Depths of My Heart" by The Isaacs
    "Glory Defined" by Building 429
    "He's an On Time God" by Dottie Peoples
    "Healer" by Kari Jobe
    "Here in Your Presence" by New Life Worship
    "Hide My Soul" by Avalon
    "Hurricane" by Natalie Grant
    "I Call You Faithful" by Donnie McClurkin
    "I Do Believe" by Steven Curtis Chapman
    "I Have a Father Who Can" by The Isaacs
    "Lord I Need You" by Matt Maher
    "Mighty to Save" by Hillsong
    "Moving All the While" by Sidewalk Prophets
    "My Hope" by Hillsong
    "Never Alone" by BarlowGirl
    "No Turning Back" by Out of Eden
    "Oceans (Where Feet May Fail)" by Hillsong United
    "One Day" by Aaron Shust
    "Over and Over" by Jeff and Sheri Easter
    "This Is Amazing Grace" by Phil Wickham
    "While I'm Waiting" by John Waller
    "You Carry Me" by Moriah Peters

Chapter 11: Finding Comfort
    "Alabaster Box" by CeCe Winans
    "All My Fountains" by Travis Cottrell
    "Every Now and Then" by FFH
    "God with Us" by MercyMe
    "Great Is Your Mercy" by Donnie McClurkin
    "Here with Me" by MercyMe
    "How Great Is Our God" by Chris Tomlin

"How I Love You" by Christy Nockels
"I Enter In" by Roger Hodges
"I Need a Healing Touch" by Heirline
"In His Hands" by The Isaacs
"Lord Send a Refuge" by Heirline
"Love Came Down" by Kari Jobe
"Never Gone" by Colton Dixon
"One True God" by Mark Harris
"The Promise" by The Martins
"Revive Me" by Jeremy Camp
"Sheltered in the Arms of God" by His Song
"Sing Me Home" by The Martins
"Through It All" by Hillsong
"Tide, Wash Over Me" by Maranatha! Promise Band
"When Mercy Found Me" by Rhett Walker Band
"You Are" by Hillsong
"You Will Never Leave Me" by Sidewalk Prophets

Chapter 12: The Courage to Continue
"The Best Is Yet To Come" by Donald Lawrence
"Call On Jesus" by Nicole C. Mullen
"Daniel" by FFH
"Do It Lord" by Travis Cottrell
"Everlasting God" by Chris Tomlin
"Faith to Believe" by Shane & Shane
"Final Chapter" by The Crabb Family
"Found a Place" by FFH
"Get Down" by Audio Adrenaline
"I'm Going to Reach Heaven" by Heirline
"I'm Not Praying to My Need" by Heirline
"If You Want Me To" by Ginny Owens
"Love Is a Cross You Bear" by The Isaacs
"Love Is the Medicine" by NewSong
"O My Soul, March On" by Travis Cottrell
"Our God" by Chris Tomlin
"Overcomer" by Mandisa

"Praise You in This Storm" by Casting Crowns
"The Presence of the Lord Is Here" by Byron Cage
"Still Holdin' On" by The Crabb Family
"Through the Valley" by The Isaacs
"Walk by Faith" by Jeremy Camp
"You Will Never Leave Me" by Sidewalk Prophets
"Your Grace Is Enough" by Chris Tomlin

Chapter 13: Spiritual Warfare (Don't Become Satan's POW)
"Above It All" by The Martins
"Alive Forever Amen" by Travis Cottrell
"Awesome God" by Maranatha! Promise Band
"Because of Who You Are" by FFH
"Blessed Assurance" by Third Day
"Ever Living God" by Hillsong
"Glory" by Hillsong
"He Reigns" by Newsboys
"Hello, My Name Is" by Matthew West
"Hosanna" by Kirk Franklin
"Hosanna in the Highest" by Passage
"I Come in the Name of the Lord" by The Isaacs
"I Have a Father Who Can" by The Isaacs
"In Christ Alone" (featuring Khristian Stanfill) by Passion
"Jesus, Son of God" (featuring Chris Tomlin and Christy Nockels) by Passion
"The Lamb, the Lion, and the King" by the Crabb Family
"More Than Amazing" by Lincoln Brewster
"On My Knees" by Nicole C. Mullen
"One True God" by NewSong
"Overcome" by Jeremy Camp
"Revelation Song" by Lindell Cooley
"The Same God" by NewSong
"Something Beautiful" by Needtobreathe
"Something Going On in the Graveyard" by The Crabb Family
"There's Only One (Holy One)" by Caedmon's Call
"Through the Fire" by The Crabb Family

"The Way" by Jeremy Camp
"When the Stars Burn Down" by Travis Cottrell
"Whom Shall I Fear (God of Angel Armies)" by Chris Tomlin
"Word of God Has Spoken" by Travis Cottrell
"You Alone" by Kutless
"You Are God Alone" by Marvin Sapp

Chapter 14: Riding the Relapse Roller Coaster
"Blessed Be Your Name" by Tree63
"By Your Side" by Tenth Avenue North
"Do It Lord" by Travis Cottrell
"East to West" by Casting Crowns
"Frontline" by Pillar
"Hear Us from Heaven" by New Life Worship
"Hold Me Now" by Jennifer Knapp
"Lay It Down" by Todd Agnew
"Made to Love" by tobyMac
"Moving all the While" by Sidewalk Prophets
"Need You Here" by Hillsong
"Need You Now (How Many Times)" by Plumb
"Pray" by Darlene Zschech
"Remember Me" by Kutless
"Revive Me" by Jeremy Camp
"The Same God" by NewSong
"Strong Enough" by Matthew West
"Strong Tower" by Kutless
"Stronger" by Mandisa
"Thrive" by Casting Crowns
"Through the Fire" by The Crabb Family
"Walk On" by The Isaacs
"What If His People Prayed" by Casting Crowns
"What If I Stumble" by DC Talk
"Whatever It Takes" by Lifehouse
"You Never Let Go" by Matt Redman
"You Save Me" by Kutless
"Your Latter Will Be Greater" by Israel & New Breed

"The Motions" by Matthew West
"Oh What A City" by Heirline
"One of These Days" by FFH
"The Promise" by The Martins
"Thank You God for Saving Me" by Chris Tomlin
"That's All That Matters to Me" by The Isaacs
"There Will Be a Day" by Jeremy Camp
"There Will Come a Day" by Faith Hill
"Though You Slay Me" by Shane & Shane
"Trust in Jesus" by Third Day
"Walk On" by the Isaacs
"Welcome Home" by Shaun Groves
"Where I Belong" by Building 429
"You Can Have Me" by Sidewalk Prophets
"10,000 Reasons (Bless the Lord)" by Matt Redman

# ABOUT THE AUTHOR

I was born in Bangor, Maine in 1966, the youngest of four girls. After my parents divorced when I was eight years old, I began going to church with my mother. A few years later, I went to live near Asheville, North Carolina with my father and stepmother and graduated from A. C. Reynolds High School in 1984. I struggled with depression, suicidal tendencies, and anger throughout my youth and on into my thirties. I quickly married at age eighteen, thinking that was the solution to my blues and that I would be happy and loved all the days of my life. It was not a happy marriage for me. We divorced eight years later. Depression and suicidal thoughts persisted, and I stopped going to church. I met my current husband, and we married a couple years later in Tennessee.

I enrolled at Middle Tennessee State University in 1994. During those college years, the truth was revealed—my new husband was a crack addict. Although I would go on to graduate with honors, magna cum laude, with a BA in communication disorders and two minors—Neuropsychology and German—the ever-present feelings of hopelessness and depression overwhelmed me. My self-esteem hit rock bottom. Thoughts of suicide loomed. My home life was a disaster. I fell to my knees before God, committing my life to him.

Having grown up in church, I believed the Bible had all of life's instructions, but I had wandered away. And although I didn't see the words "cocaine" or "crack" in the Bible, I believed the answers were in there. I began searching, studying God's Word, and finding what I needed for every question and problem. Over the next several years, depression, low self-esteem, and hopelessness lost their grip on me. Through God's Word I also discovered how to deal with my husband and his addiction. I never knew for certain that he would quit using drugs, but I no longer tethered myself to his pendulum. I found myself secure on the rock that is higher than I, becoming more than an overcomer through Christ my Lord!

My husband and I survived, only by the grace of God, and recently celebrated our twentieth wedding anniversary. I became a flight attendant for Southwest Airlines in 1999, and Lonnie has been clean for about fourteen years now. We are very happy and more in love than ever. We currently live in the countryside, outside of Nashville, TN, with our seventeen-year-old grandson, Lonnie Lee. I teach an adult Sunday school class at my local church. My husband and I enjoy playing music at church and at home. Lonnie plays guitar, I play piano, and am learning to play the cello. Lonnie Lee is learning to play the drums. We started a nonprofit called Heart of Hosea Ministries, through which we help addicts, the homeless, and the less privileged on an as-need basis and send monthly support to a small orphanage in Kenya. You may find more information about us on the web at HeartofHosea.org. We would love for you to partner with us! All contributions are tax exempt. We covet your prayers!

It is my calling, my passion, to teach others the Word of God— the gospel message of Jesus Christ—in practical and powerful ways, which permanently alter their landscape. God's Word has a genuine, transformative power like none other! This is my first published book, but I have written much over the years while teaching the Bible to adults and dealing with others who, like us, lived messy lives. I look forward to publishing more in the future!

CPSIA information can be obtained at www.ICGtesting.com
Printed in the USA
LVOW12s0036300914

406398LV00003B/7/P